\<\<Bird View\>\>

I0423509

For information contact: www.beizhanliu.com

Book Cover and Back Cover Photo Created by Dario Sanches
(https://flic.kr/p/8N5UQN)

ISBN 978-1505482515

CreateSpace.com

First Edition: December 2014

Dedication

For you, the world we love forever

For you, the life we love forever

For you, the peace we love forever

For you, the equal we love forever

<<Bird View>>

Preface

From south to north, from east to west, the similarity of all things in the world, the difference of people's lives, often cause my reveries and laments. The ever lasting is this small globe we inhabit; the ephemerally fleeting is our brilliant and helpless life. In the end what kind life shall we have? In the end what kind world shall we have? In the end how shall we look at so many things ever happened or are happening in this world? I dreamed I was the little bird away from the hubbub flying in the air, overlooking this small globe, writing my reveries with my pen, engraving my laments with my pen, and I would like to be able to contribute some slight forces for the improvement of this world with my reveries, I would like to provide a little faint light for people to enjoy a happy life with my laments.

Time flies, beyond my thought, dozens of articles had accumulated in just more than one year. Now they are collected in this book to be published. The mainly related topics of this book are: **World security, Asia security, diplomatic relations, diplomatic aid strategy, international relations, international interventionism, globalization, international dispute resolution strategy, Israeli-Palestinian relation, the former Yugoslavia, India and China relation, energy and energy policy, the North American energy security strategy, the innovation capability and competitiveness of United States and Canada, immigration management and policy making, political party management, modern legislative system, legal document writing principle, President Lyndon**

Johnson, the future of internet and its management, technology innovation, decision making theory, workflow management, leadership, China's legal system history, the history of Chinese people, the spirit of America, religion, business, history, culture, education, family relationship, love relationship, the phenomenon of single families in North America, and so on.

I think a lot of views I advocated are very new, very realistic. It shall be more effective for world management and security management. This book should be a good book to open up thoughts for those who are interested in international relations, international security, politics, political party, legal and policy development, scientific management and decision-making, and so on. This book will also be more helpful for those who have already engaged in and who want to engage in **political work, government work, diplomatic work, social work or management work**; because I think most strategies and ideas proposed in this book will eventually be accepted by most countries in the world.

Finally, "**Let us give up the World War II thinking, and build up the relationship between countries with our new vision, work together to build up we all owned the spacecraft sailing in the space.**"

从南到北，从东到西，世界万物之相形，人世沧桑之不同，时常引起我的遐思与慨叹。亘古不变的是我们所居住的这个小小的寰球，转瞬即逝的是我们灿烂又无奈的人生。我们到底应该拥有什么样的人生？我们到底应该拥有一个什么样的世界？我们到底应该如何看待这个世界曾经发生的和正在发生的许多事情？小小的我梦想我就是那一只远离尘嚣，翱翔在空中的小鸟，俯瞰这个小小的寰球，用我的笔记起我的遐思，刻下我的慨叹，并愿我的遐思能为这个世界的完善尽一点些微的力量，愿我的慨叹能为人们享有幸福的生活供一点微弱的光亮。

时光荏苒，不曾想，积少成多，仅一年多的时间，就已积累了几十篇。现收集在此文集中出版。这篇文集主要涉及到的议题有：世界安全，亚洲安全，外交关系，外交援助策略，国际关系，国际干涉主义，全球一体化，国际争议解决策略，以色列和巴勒斯坦关系，前南斯拉夫问题，印度和中国的关系，能源及能源政策，北美能源安全策略，美国与加拿大的创新力和竞争力，移民管理及政策制定，政党管理，现代立法制度，法律文件起草原则，林顿约翰逊总统，互联网的未来及其管理，科技创新，决策理论，工作流管理，领袖才能，中国的法制历史，中国人的历史，美国精神，宗教，商业，历史，文化，教育，家庭关系，爱情关系，北美单身家庭现象，等等。

我认为我提出的很多观点都是很崭新的，很现实的。对于世界管理和安全管理来讲，应该是比较有效的。这本文集对于那些对国际关系，国际安全，政治，政党，法律及政策制定，科学管理及决策，等等感兴趣的人士应该是一本比较好的开拓思维的读本。对于从事和希望从事**政治工作，政府工作，外交工作，社会工作或管理工作**的人士也是比较有帮助的，因为我认为这本文集所提出的很多方案和观点最终必将为世界上大多数的国家所接受。

最后"**让我们摒弃二战思维，以新的视野来构建国与国之间的关系，共同打造这艘我们共有的航行在太空中的宇宙飞船**"。

Author Bio

 The Author Beizhan Liu is a Chinese Canadian who lives in Toronto, Canada. He is an enterpriser, innovator and visionary. He invented VRP (Video Reality Processing) technology. He created Query Interview (QI) Communication Platform – WorldIntervieW.net which is the third way to communicate on the internet with message. He is also a seasonal recruiter. He has a background in science research and software engineering. He loves photography and music. He has broad interests in management, international issue, politics, foreign relation, legislature, government, education, religion, culture, economy, etc. This book is a collection of his spare weekend writing from June 12, 2013 to October 16, 2014 which includes total 55 articles. Some innovative concepts to shape our world are proposed in this book, such as: Asian Union, Asia Security Council, Internet Kingdom, Internet Citizenship, Internet Passport, Solution for Israel and Palestine Conflict, Solution for Cross Border Resource Disputation, etc. He is also a talent of management. His detailed experiences on decision making, policy making, conflict resolving, workflow management, etc. are also presented in this book. He loves life no matter in what kind situations. He advocates quality life and presents his feeling in his articles. He has a beautiful wife Amy Jiang who passed away in April of 2003.

<<Bird View>>

Acknowledgement

Thank you Amy for your spiritual support with God!

Table of Contents

Solutions for Wrong Decision

[错误决定的解决方案]

In our work and life, we are always making this or that decision. Whether it is a personal decision or a team decision, in most situations our decision may be correct, but in individual situation, our decision may be wrong. So, when we find that our decision may be wrong, what kind action should we take? This is what I want to talk about **the solution to the wrong decision**.

<<Bird View>>

Solution to the wrong decision shall include the following contents:

1). Policy makers shall dare to face mistake and admit mistake with frank feeling;

2). Policy makers shall **double verify the wrong decision** in order to avoid cognitive mistake;

3). Policy makers shall take a positive attitude to make the decision again and try to recover the losses brought by the wrong decision;

4). When decision makers make the decision again, **the revisable solution** for the original wrong decision shall be considered firstly;

5). When decision makers make decision again, **the no-cost alternative solution** shall be considered secondly;

6). When decision makers make decision again, **the low-cost alternative solution** can also be considered;

7). When decision makers make decision again, they shall **double confirm the correctness of the new decision** in order to avoid cognitive mistakes;

8). Regarding the wrong decision which cannot be corrected or the decision can not be made again, we only have to take the lesson, summarize the experience, and try to avoid the recurrence of such similar wrong decision.

For example: In commercial contracts, some contracts often have liquidated damage clause. In case of such contracts belonging to the wrong decisions, it may take the measure of **contract extension, contract replacement with guaranteed benefits in order to avoid compensation for breach of contract**, so that the interests of both contract parties can be assured when the decision is made again.

In short, the wrong decision should be avoided, although sometimes it is inevitable. When decision makers make decision again while facing the wrong decision, they shall think twice before take action and try to avoid or recover the damage caused by the wrong decision.

在我们的工作和生活中，我们总是在不断地作出这样或那样的决定。无论是个人的决定抑或是集体的决定，在多数的情况下，我们的决定可能是正确的，但在个别情况下，我们的决定也可能是错误的。 那么，当我们发现我们的决定可能是错误的时候，我们又该如何行动呢？这就是我要谈的**错误决定的解决方案**。

错误决定的解决方案应当包含以下几点内容：

1）。决策者要敢于以坦然的心情面对错误，并承认错误；

2）。决策者要以**双重证实的方式认定决定的错误**以避免认知上的错误；

3）。决策者要以积极的态度进行再次的决策，并尽力挽回错误决定所带来的损失；

4）。决策者再次决策时，首先要考虑对原错误决定**可修改**的解决方案；

5）。决策者再次决策时，其次要考虑**无代价的可替代的解决方案**；

6）。决策者再次决策时，还可以考虑**代价较小的可替代的解决方案**；

7）。决策者再次决策时，还要以**双重证实的方式认定新决定的正确性**以避免认知上的错误；

8）。对于无法修正或无法再次决策的错误决定，只有吸取教训，总结经验，避免类似的错误决定的再次发生；

例如：在商业合同中，有的合同常有毁约赔偿条款，当此种合同属于错误决定的情形下，不妨**采取延期，利益保证下的合同更换等方式**来避免毁约的赔偿，从而使合同双方的利益在再次决策时得到保证。

总之，错误决定应当尽量避免，尽管有时在所难免。决策者面对错误决定再次决策时，一定要三思而后行，并尽量避免或挽回错误决定所带来的损失。

Thursday, October 16, 2014

4

On The Hierarchy of Decision Making

[论决策的层次性]

After talking about the relationship between science decision-making and democratic decision-making, I would like to talk further about the hierarchy of decision making. Whether democratic decision-making or scientific decision making, they all are hierarchical in nature, which is determined by the internal logic relation of the right decision. Decision-making hierarchy is the systematic manifestation of decision, is the perfect performance of decision. Decision-making hierarchy is actually an alternative expression of scientific nature of decision-making.

1). Decision-making hierarchy firstly manifested in that the decision-making object is hierarchical;

2). Decision-making hierarchy secondly manifested in that the importance (or priority) of the decision-making objects is hierarchical;

3). Decision-making hierarchy thirdly manifested in that the decision making process is hierarchical;

4). Decision-making hierarchy is also reflected in that the content of the decision-making is hierarchical;

5). Decision-making hierarchy is also reflected in that the decision-making support system is hierarchical;

6). Decision-making hierarchy is also reflected in that the decision-making logic reasoning process is hierarchical;

7). Decision-making hierarchy is also reflected in that decision-makers are hierarchical in team decision-making;

Understanding the decision-making hierarchy can achieve effective decision management, which do produce the maximum possibility to avoid wrong decision, and to ensure a perfect decision-making, and to improve the decision-making efficiency at the same time.

在谈过了科学决策和民主决策的关系之后，我想再进一步谈一谈决策的层次性问题。无论是科学决策还是民主决策，都是有层次性的，这也是正确决策的内在逻辑关系所决定的。决策的层次性是决策的系统性的表现，是决策完美性的表现。决策的层次性其实也是决策科学性的另类体现。

1）。决策的层次性首先表现在决策对象是有层次的；

2）。决策的层次性其次表现在决策对象的重要性（或优先权）是有层次的；

3）。决策的层次性再次表现在决策的过程是有层次性的；

4）。决策的层次性还表现在决策的内容是有层次性的；

5）。决策的层次性也表现在决策的支持系统是有层次性的；

6）。决策的层次性还表现在决策的逻辑推理过程是有层次性的；

7）。决策的层次性也表现在集体决策的决策者是有层次性的；

了解决策的层次性，可以实现有效的决策管理，从而尽最大可能的避免错误决策的产生，并保证决策的完美性，同时还可以提高决策效率。

Sunday, October 5, 2014

Global Interest and Local Interest

[全局利益与局部利益]

What do we see when we see a peacock is opening her wing? What we see is a beautiful peacock with huge straighten wing, what we see is that there are so many gems like markings on the wing. Here we not only see **the beauty of the whole peacock**, but also see **the peacock's local beauty**. So the relationship between global interest and local interest is like the wing's opening of peacock, must be coordinated to develop, to achieve the best result.

The differences of global interest and local interest reflect in all aspects of our society, this is **the level of social interest**. For example: the interest of a country as a whole comparing with the interest of a province within this country is global interest, however the interest of each province is local interest; The interest of a city as a whole comparing with the interest of a community within the city is global interest, however the interest of each community is local interest. The interest of an interest body at the level of social interest can be global interest on one hand and can be local interest on the other hand due to different corresponding interest body. This is **the relativity of social interest**.

In the process of accessing social resource by global interest and local interest, they may diminish the importance of each other. This is **the rivalry of social interest**. When the importance of global interest is greater than that of local interest or when global interest is a support to local interest, the priority of global interest is greater than the priority of local interest. When the importance of local interest is greater than that of global interest or when local interest is an important component of the global interest, the priority of local interest is greater than the priority of global interest. **This is the priority of the social interest.** At the same time global interest and local interest have mutual supporting and mutual constitution relationships. This is **the coordination of social interest.**

When considering the distribution of social interest based on the difference of global interest and local interest, **be sure to coordinate the relationship between global interest and local interest well.** If **the overall situation needs to be considered**, we must give priority to the global interest. When the importance of certain local interest is over other local interests even the global interest, we need to give priority to that local interest.

当我们看到孔雀开屏时，我们看到了什么？我们看到的是挺起巨大羽翼的美丽的孔雀，我们看到的是羽翼上那像一颗颗宝石似的斑纹。这里我们既看到了孔雀**整体的美**，也看到了孔雀**局部的美**。那么全局利益和局部利益的关系就像孔雀开屏一样，一定要协调发展，才会取得最好的结果。

全局利益和局部利益的不同体现在社会的方方面面，这也就是**社会利益的层次性**。例如：一个国家整体的利益对于这个国家内的一个省份的利益来讲就是全局的利益，而各个省份的利益就是局部的利益。一个城市整体的利益对于这个城市内的一个社区的利益来讲就是全局的利益，而各个社区的利益就是局部的利益。一个利益体的利益在社会利益的层次当中由于相对应的利益体的不同可能一方面是全局利益，另一方面却是局部利益。这就是**社会利益的相对性**。

全局利益和局部利益在获取社会资源的过程中，有可能会相互削弱对方的重要性。这也就是**社会利益的竞争性**。当全局利益的重要性大于局部利益或当全局利益是局部利益的支撑时，全局利益的优先权就大于局部利益的优先权。当局部利益的重要性大于全局利益或当局部利益是全局利益的重要组成时，局部利益的优先权就大于全局利益的优先权。这也就是**社会利益的优先权**。全局利益和局部利益同时具有相互支撑和相互构成的关系。这也就是**社会利益的协调性**。

在基于全局利益和局部利益的区别下考虑社会利益分配时，一定要协调好全局利益和局部利益的关系。需要顾全大局的情况下，一定要优先考虑全局利益。当某一局部利益的重要性超越其他局部利益甚至全局利益的情况下，就需要优先考虑此局部利益。(Tuesday, September 30, 2014)

The Concepts of Internet Kingdom and Internet Citizenship

［网络王国与网络公民的概念］

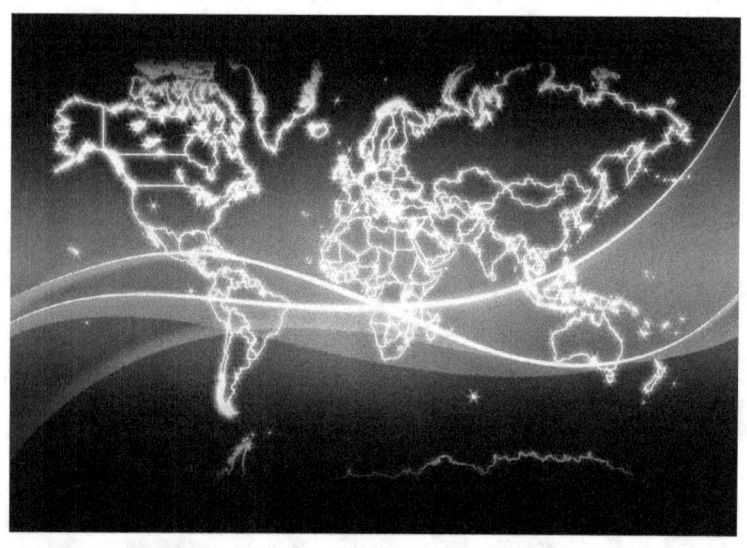

I still remember I said in 2001 that **our internet was still immature, still in early childhood**. Ten more years later, what is **the status of our internet**? Firstly the development and usage of the internet are still not balanced; network security issues remain the same; authenticity issue of the internet user's identity, simplicity issue of internet usage, and so on are not resolved, that means our internet has not much improvements. So, how to make our internet thrive **from early childhood into the youth age**?

Each of us on this planet is affiliated with a particular country, with a citizen (or resident) identification. So I think that on the internet, the concept of country can be extended, every country has the right to manage their own internet territory, to establish and expand their internet kingdom, to develop their own internet citizens and issue internet passports. Internet Citizen is the user or visitor of the internet assets associated with a country (state, enterprises and individuals). These are the concepts of Internet Kingdom and Internet Citizen I would like to propose.

I think this is a whole new thinking, because it is a management model based on the country level across the world. Historically, Microsoft has proposed passport email service which is a simple authentication and registration method for multi-service system based on one company. So it has quite a lot of differences with the concept of Internet Passport related with the Internet Citizen that I proposed.

Based on the concepts of Internet Kingdom and Internet Citizen I proposed, we can achieve the following aspects of meanings:

1). Country Form - The concept of Internet Kingdom can let a small country to be a superpower country;

2). Country Competition Form - The concept of Internet Kingdom can make the competition among countries to be over the geographic limitation, the competition will be more equitable;

3). **Society** - The concept of Internet Citizen makes a country's social structure to extend to every corner of the world, **a country's society will be divided into two levels**: the society composed of citizens living in the local and the society composed of internet citizens;

4). **Security** - The concept of Internet Passport allows us to achieve **an orderly and precise management**, thus providing maximum security for us;

5). **International Management** - The concept of Internet Passport can solve the authenticity issue of internet user's identification completely, so as to provide the most effective tool for international management, such as: business management, security management, anti-terrorism, etc.;

6). **Simplicity** - The concept of Internet Passport will greatly simplify the process of registration and authentication process when using the internet services, thus providing more simplicity for us;

7). **Finance** - The concept of Internet Kingdom can let the public administration departments of a country to get huge economic returns with simple, low-cost services, even if the price is only one dollar;

In summary, based on my thoughts, our internet thus will enter **the era of orderly management with fair competition**. Thus **the concept of country** will be changed, **the form of country competition** will also thereby be changed. I wish all the people of the world can remember today and begin to work together to upgrade our Internet and expand everyone's own Internet Kingdom, thus improving **our shared spaceship**.

我依然记得在 2001 年的时候我曾经说过我们的**互联网还很稚嫩，还处于幼儿时代**。十几年过去了，我们的**互联网的现状**是什么呢？首先是互联网的发展和利用依然处于不平衡的状态；网络安全的问题依然如故；网络用户身份的真实性问题，网络使用的简易化问题，等等均未得到解决，也就是说我们的互联网并未有太大的完善。那么，如何使我们的互联网茁壮成长，由幼儿时代进入青年时代呢？

我们在这个地球上的每一个人都是隶属于某一个国家的，都有一个公民（或居民）的身份。 那么我认为在**互联网上，国家的概念应该予以延伸**，每一个国家都有权利管理自己的互联网领土，建立和拓展自己的网络王国，发展自己的网络公民和颁发自己的网络护照。网络公民就是一个国家的与互联网相关的网络资产（国家，企业和个人）的使用者或访问者。这就是我所提出的网络王国和网络公民的概念。

我认为这是一个全新的概念，因为这是一个世界范围内的基于国家层次的管理模式。在历史上，微软曾经提出的**护照电邮**服务只是基于一个公司的多服务系统的简单注册认证方法。因此与我所提出的网络公民相关的**网络护照**的概念是有很大区别的。

基于我所提出的**网络王国和网络公民**的概念，我们可以实现以下几个方面的意义：

1）。**国家形态－网络王国的概念使得小国一样可以成为超级大国**；

２）。**国家竞争形态**－网络王国的概念使得国家竞争可以完全超越地理的限制，**竞争更为公平**；

３）。**社会**－网络公民的概念使得一个国家的社会结构延伸至世界的各个角落，**一个国家的社会将被分成两个层面**：即居于本土的公民所构成的社会和网络公民所构成的社会；

４）。**安全**－网络护照的概念可以使我们实现**对互联网的有序和精确的管理**，从而为我们提供最高的安全性；

５）。**国际管理**－网络护照的概念可以完全解决网络用户身份的真实性问题，从而为国际管理，例如：商业管理，安全管理，反恐，等等，提供最有效的工具；

６）。**简易性 ——** 网络护照的概念将大大简化使用网络服务时的各种注册和认证的过程，从而为我们提供更多的简易性；

７）。**财经 ——** 网络王国的概念使得各国的公共管理部门可以以简单，低价的服务获得巨额的经济回报，即使价格仅为一块钱；

总之，基于我的思想，互联网由此将进入**公平竞争的有序管理时代**。**国家的概念**将由此改变，**国家竞争的形态**也将由此改变。但愿世界上所有的人都能够记住今天并开始共同努力升级我们的互联网，拓展各自的网络王国，从而完善我们共有的**宇宙飞船**。

Sunday, September 14, 2014

Democratic Decision-Making and Scientific Decision-Making

［民主决策与科学决策］

In my previous article, I talked the details about scientific decision-making and the relationship between scientific decision-making and workflow management. Here I want to talk about **democratic decision-making and the relationship between democratic decision-making and scientific   decision-making.**

<<Bird View>>

Democratic decision-making is a more common decision-making mode in everyday life, in political life, it is even more common. Democratic election in the West is the most typical expression of democratic decision-making mode. **Democratic decision-making refers to the collective decision-makers make decision by a simple majority of voting directly or indirectly. Democratic decision-making is generally applied to the decision on people or activities of people or is applied to the decision on things at the final developing period.** Democratic decision-making generally goes through the process of fully conveying the information of decision-making object to the decision makers, the interactive process of decision-making object or the owner of the decision-making object with decision makers, the assessment and argument process for decision-makers to the decision-making object, the decision-making process for the decision-makers on the decision-making object. In democratic decision-making, if the decision-making object is a solution for a complex system, then usually it is needed to use scientific means to form and proof such solution, which is contributed to the final decision of the decision-maker. Democratic decision-making will also involve system engineering, workflow management, and so on. Democratic decision-making in most cases is a simple and easy to be accepted decision-making mode, the correctness of this decision-making mode can be guaranteed in most cases either. But if in case of poor information, less assessment, or unfair decision-makers, democratic decision-making will deviate from the right track.

Scientific decision-making generally is used in large complex system, which can use scientific methods to obtain data based on facts, and on this basis to form the final decision. Normally democratic decision-making is needed to be supported by scientific decision-making, such as: solution formation, comparison and assessment of decision result, and so on. However, scientific decision-making does not require too much democratic decision-making ingredient, of course, the result of scientific decision-making has to conform to the common needs of decision makers.

In short, it is better to grasp the application of democratic decision-making and scientific decision-making well in reality. Thus we can ensure the correctness of decision-making to the greatest possibility.

在我的前一篇文章中，我详细的谈到了科学决策以及科学决策与工作流管理的关系。这里我想谈一谈民主决策以及民主决策和科学决策之间的关系。

民主决策在日常生活中是比较常见的决策方式，在政治生活中，则更为普遍。西方的民主选举就是民主决策的最典型的表现。民主决策是指集体决策者直接的或间接的以简单多数的投票表决方式所进行的决策。民主决策一般应用于与人或人的活动相关的决策或应用于事物发展终端阶段的决策。民主决策一般要经过决策对象信息向决策者完全传达的过程，决策对象或决策对象所有人与决策者互动的过程，决策者对决策对象评估论证的过程，决策者对决策对象的决策过程。在民主决策中如果决策对象是某种复杂系统的解决方案，则往往要经由科学的手段来形成并论证此方案，并促成决策者的最终决定。民主决策中一样会涉及到系统工程，工作流管理，等等。民主决策在大多数情况下是一种简单的易于为人所接受的决策方式，其决策的正确性在大多数的情况下也是能够得到保证的。 但如果在信息不畅，论证不够，或决策人有失公平的情况下，民主决策就会偏离正确的轨道。

科学决策一般应用于复杂的大系统，能够利用科学手段获得基于事实的数据，并在此基础之上做出最终的决策。民主决策常常需要科学决策的支持，例如：解决方案的形成，决策结果的比较与论证，等等。科学决策却不需要太多的民主决策的成分，当然科学决策的结果还是要顺应决策者的共同的需要的。

总之，在现实中要把握好民主决策与科学决策的应用。从而尽最大的可能保证决策的正确性。

Sunday, September 7, 2014

Workflow Management and Immigration Policy

[工作流管理和移民政策]

Workflow management should also be given adequate attention in the formulation of immigration policy, and should be applied to it. Workflow management can produce the following benefits in the formulation of immigration policy:

1). Build a clear and simple workflow

2). Remove duplicated intermediate links

3). Save time and money for applicants

4). Save time and money for government and country

5). Realize the minimized filings and documents

6). Reduce the filing and document storage space and circulation links as most as possible

The application of workflow management in immigration policy formulation is reflected specifically in two respects:

legal immigration management and illegal immigration management:

1). Legal Immigration Management

In designing the workflow for processing legal immigration, the principles of **local (insider) priority and student priority** shall be considered, which are based on the consideration of local life experiences and expenses. **Repeated application process shall be revised to a single application process which employer can be updated. The buffer like indirect immigration application process guided by immigration authorities shall be revised to the direct immigration application process guided by employers,** thereby clearing **the resource consumption, time wasting** and **the battles between departments** brought by the buffer.

2). Illegal Immigration Management

In designing the workflow for processing illegal immigration, firstly it is needed to understand a few basic concepts. First, **illegal immigrants should be equivalent to the inside foreigners**. Second, illegal immigrants can probably be divided into two types: one is **obstructed resource flow**, one is **injected resource flow**. Of course, illegal immigration shall not be encouraged. Trying to prevent the entry of illegal immigrants shall be the first. But for inside foreigners, **the principles of employer decision and local labor market decision** shall be considered, **which are based on the consideration for acquiring value of** social stability, value of economic stability and value of **humanitarian.** Another principle to be considered is that **the inside foreigners shall have the right to obtain legal visas as outside foreigners.** Of course, illegal inside foreigners have the obligation to pay economic compensation for their illegal behaviors, their political rights shall also be treated differently, so as to discourage the injected resource flow based on political factors, and gradually get the phenomenon of illegal immigration to be completely controlled.

In fact, **immigration work shall be treated as the exploration work for domestic and foreign talent resource and labor resource**; it is a **human resource work** in a special area with more extensiveness. Under such a premise, applying the workflow management to the formulation of immigration policy will have rules to follow up.

工作流管理在移民政策的制定中，也应当给与足够的重视，并加以应用。工作流管理在移民政策中的应用可以起到以下几个方面的作用：

1）。构筑简单清晰的工作流程

2）。去除重复的中间环节

3）。为申请人节省时间和金钱

4）。为政府和国家节省时间和金钱

5）。实现文档的最小化

6）。最大可能的减少文档的存储空间和流通环节

工作流管理在移民政策中的应用可以具体的体现在**合法移民管理和非法移民管理**两个方面：

1）。合法移民

在处理合法移民的工作流设计中应当考虑**本地(内部)优先**和**学生优先**的原则，这是基于对本地生活经验和成本的考虑。**重复的申请流程应当修改为雇主可更新的单一申请流程。**由移民部门所主导的非直接的缓存器似的移民申请流程应当修改为雇主所主导的直接的移民申请流程，从而清除缓存器所带来的**资源消耗，时间的浪费及部门的争斗。**

2）。非法移民

在处理非法移民的工作流设计中，首先要搞清楚几个基本的概念。第一，**非法移民应当等同于境内外国人。**第二，非法移民大概可以分成两种：一种是属于**受阻的资源流**，一种是**注射的资源流。**非法移民当然不应当是被鼓励的。尽量阻止非法移民的进入应当是第一位的。但对于境内外国人来讲，应当考虑**雇主决定原则和本地劳工市场决定原则**，这是基于取得社会稳定的价值，经济稳定的价值以及人道主义的价值而考虑的。另外一个 要考虑的原则就是**境内外国人应当同境外外国人一样有权利获得合法的签证。**当然非法的境内外国人也有义务为非法的行为付出经济上的赔偿，在政治权利上也应当被区别对待，从而达到不鼓励基于政治因素的注射资源流，使得非法移民现象逐步得到彻底的控制。

其实，**移民的工作应当看作是对于境内外智力资源和劳工资源的挖掘的工作；**是一个特殊领域的又较具广泛性的人力资

源的工作。在这样一个大前提下，将工作流管理应用到移民政策制定中也就有章可循了。

Tuesday, August 26, 2014

Giving Up the Thinking of World War II, Building Up Relationship between Countries with New Vision

[摒弃二战思维，以新的视野构建国与国之间的关系]

World War II had ended for a long time, but the war did not disappear on this earth since then. After World War II, we have experienced a number of regional wars, for example: the Korean War, the Vietnam War, the many times wars in Afghanistan, many times wars in the Middle East, the war in the former Yugoslavia, the Iran-Iraq war, the Iraq war, as well as the recent Libya war and the civil war in Syria, and so on. Every war seems to remind people that **the World War II has not ended, it continues. This is so called the World War II thinking. World War II thinking always thinks that the World War**

II has not ended, always emphasizes the **confrontation factor between countries, the confrontation factor between groups of countries, thereby generating the above all safety point of view.** Is our real world really like this? Is the future of our social reality truly like this? This relates to the issue of **relationships among countries** and the issue of **world structure** built on such relationships.

The relationship between countries first is the relation of cooperation and development, a cooperation and development relationship on the basis of mutual trust. Especially for areas neighboring countries concerned, it is even more so. Due to historical reasons, territory reasons, religious reasons, ideological reasons, and so on, **confrontation** between countries or groups of countries exists, but **should not be the first one, and should not be encouraged, but should be eased and eliminated.**

On the issue of world structure, some people advocate **unipolar world**, some people advocate **multi-polar world.** In my opinion, our world is neither a unipolar world nor a multi-polar world, but **a balanced developed world.** You may have seen the cartoon movie **<<WAR-E>>,** our world itself is, like the metaphor by some people, **a spacecraft sailing in the space,** which is an inevitable result due to **the economic globalization and the information globalization.** Only with a balanced development, it will not let our spaceship   overturning   capsized.

World War II brought a huge disaster to the people of the world. People in many countries have paid a huge price in human lives. Of course there are many countries made great contributions to end the World War II. Nevertheless, World War II was over, we can not have either too much **attitude of gratitude**, or too much **revenge mentality. Let us give up the World War II thinking, and build up the relationship between countries with our new vision, work together to build up we all owned the spacecraft sailing in the space.**

第二次世界大战早已结束了，然而战争却并没有在这个地球上就此消失。在二战之后我们又经历了多次的地区性战争，例如：韩战，越战，多次的阿富汗战争，多次的中东战争，前南斯拉夫战争，两伊战争，伊拉克战争，还有最近的利比亚之战和叙利亚内战，等等。每次战争的发生都让人觉得似乎二战尚未结束，仍在继续。这就是所谓的二战的思维。

二战的思维总是认为二战尚未结束，总是强调国与国之间对抗的因素，国家集团与国家集团之间对抗的因素，由此产生大于一切的安全观点。难道我们的现实世界真的是这样的吗？难道我们现实社会的未来真的是这样的吗？这就涉及到一个**国家关系**的问题和一个建立在此关系之上的**世界结构**的问题。

国家关系首先是合作与发展的关系，是建立在相互信任基础之上的合作与发展的关系。尤其是对于地域相邻的国家来讲，更是如此。由于历史的原因，领土的原因，宗教的原因，意识形态的原因，等等，国与国之间的**对抗**或国家集团与国家集团之间的对抗是存在的，**但不应该是第一位的，更不应该是被鼓励的，而应当是被缓和和被消除的。**

对于**世界结构**的问题，有人主张**单极的世界**，有人主张**多极的世界**。在我看来，我们的世界既不是单极的世界，也不是多极的世界，而应当是一个**平衡发展的世界**。大家也许都看过动画片《**WAR-E**》，我们的世界就像某些人所比喻的那样，其本身就是**航行在太空中的一艘宇宙飞船**，这是由于**经济全球化和信息全球化**所导致的必然结果。只有平衡发展，才不致于使我们这艘宇宙飞船倾覆翻船。

二战给世界人民带来巨大的灾难。许多国家的人民都付出了巨大的生命代价。当然也有许多国家为二战的结束做出了巨大的贡献。但无论如何，二战已经结束了，我们既不可以有太多**报恩的心态**，更不可以有太多**复仇的心态**。**让我们摒弃二战思维，以新的视野来构建国与国之间的关系，共同打造这艘我们共有的航行在太空中的宇宙飞船。**

Saturday, August 16, 2014

Scientific Decision-Making and Work Flow Management

[科学决策与工作流管理]

Due to the development of information technology and the development of scaled economy in modern society, it makes our management work to have a growing need for scientific decision-making practices. Scientific decision-making is defined relatively to the experience decision-making. **Scientific decision-making means that the decision makers make decision based on the reality of**

decision objects (projects, engineering projects, etc.) with the utilization of scientific means (methods, models and tools, etc.). Elements of scientific decision-making lie in scientific decision-making processes, scientific decision-making means and the means for the implementation of the scientific decision-making.

Scientific decision-making is clearly inseparable with workflow management. **Workflow refers to the integration of all work units which can be decomposed from any one task or job and their relationships. Workflow management is to optimize workflow by applying scientific methods in order to improve the work productivity.** In scientific decision-making, workflow **management involves three areas: workflow management of the decision-making process, workflow management of the decision object and workflow management of the decision-making implementation process.** Only with a complete workflow management system, will we achieve real scientific decision-making.

In reality, due to the lack of workflow management practice, decision-making behavior lacks scientific aspect, often appears as indecisive decision, decision without implementation, repeated decision-making or hasty decision, blind decision phenomenon, and result in enormous losses to our society and our country. Such phenomenon is repeated to appear and is not fresh. Therefore, it is necessary to emphasize the importance of workflow management in scientific decision-making. Decision-making built up on the workflow management can only be called as true scientific decision-making, and **will ensure maximum rightness of the decision-making** while achieving the purpose of improving work productivity.

现代社会由于信息化的发展和规模经济的发展，使得我们的管理工作日益需要科学决策的实践。科学决策是相对于经验决策而言的。**科学决策是指决策者基于决策对象（项目，工程项目，等等）的现实，运用科学手段（方法，模式和工具，等等）所进行的决策。科学决策的要素在于科学的决策流程，科学的决策手段以及科学的决策实施手段。**

科学决策同工作流管理显然是密不可分的。**工作流是指完成任何一项工作或任务所可分解的任务单元及相互关系的集成。工作流管理是指运用科学手段优化工作流以提高工作效率。在科学决策中，工作流管理涉及到三个方面：决策过程的工作流管理，决策对象的工作流管理和决策实施过程的工作流管理。**只有具备完备的工作流管理体系，才会实现真正的科学决策。

在现实社会中，由于缺乏工作流管理的实践，决策行为缺乏科学化，常常出现议而不决，决而不行，反复决策或仓促决策，盲目决策的现象，结果给社会和国家带来巨大的损失。这种现象屡见不鲜。因此，很有必要强调工作流管理在科学决策中的重要性。建立在工作流管理之上的决策才能够称得上是真正的科学决策，才会**最大限度的保证决策的正确性，**并同时实现提高工作效率的目的。

Monday, August 4, 2014

<<Bird View>>

Perfect Business Suite

[完美的商业包装]

In the development of modern business, the business suite has become a very important component in the modern business society. Almost all business activities in every country and every industry are inseparable from business suite. Most people think that business suite refers to packaging of goods or the packaging of business environment. In fact, this understanding is not complete. In my opinion, **business suite should be defined as follows: In order to meet the general consensus of the business community, in order to establish a good business image, in order to promote sales, business (or government and service organizations in the society) takes suites on or**

packages for or regulation for goods or services, business facilities, commercial practitioners, or the business activities carried out.

Further more business development is actually a kind business suite development. Especially in today's information society, business suiting presents throughout all aspects of commercial circulation, from commercial brands to commercial websites, from commercial websites to social media, from social media to online payment, from merchants to owners, from owners to employees, from employees to customers, from government to government officials, from officials to the people. The business suiting is developing while creating a lot of new businesses.

Business activities have to achieve its business values with a suitable business suite. Business suite is a necessary bridge between business and customers for business to deliver their products or services. However, over emphasizing on business suite is contrary to the nature of the business activities. In social reality, this phenomenon is **not uncommon in the cart before the horse.** Business suiting is not only related to the cost of business, but also more related to the environment and resources especially for product packaging concerned. Over packaging or luxury packaging of goods may bring huge waste for the society and the consumer, and therefore should not be encouraged.

Perfect business activities require perfect business suite. However, after all, business is the substance of business, and therefore we must not **stop feeding because of choking**, hinder the development of business, or give up business opportunities because of business suiting. So, **the perfect business activities actually require a suitable business suite.**

在现代商业的发展中，商业包装已经成为现代商业社会中非常重要的一个组成部分。几乎每一个国家，每一个行业的商业活动都离不开商业包装。 大多数人认为商业包装指的就是商品的包装或商业环境的包装，其实这种认识是不完全的。在我看来，**商业包装应该定义为：为适应商业社会的普遍共识，为树立良好的商业形象，为促进商品或服务的销售，商家（或政府及社会服务机构）对商品或服务，商业设施，商业从业人员及商业活动所进行的包装或规范。**

商业的发展其实更多的是商业包装的发展. 尤其是在当今的信息社会，商业包装贯穿于商业流通的各个方面， 从商业品牌，到商业网站，从商业网站到社交媒体，从社交媒体到网络支付，从商家到所有人，从所有人到雇员，从雇员到客户，从政府到官员，从官员到百姓。 而商业包装的发展同时也创造了许许多多的新型商业。

商业活动是要以合适的商业包装来实现其商业价值的。商业包装则是商家将产品或服务传送到用户的一个必要的桥梁。 然而，过于强调商业包装却是有悖于商业活动的本质的。在现实社会中，这种本末倒置的现象是**屡见不鲜**的。 商业包装不仅涉及到商业成本，更涉及到环境及资源，尤其是就产品包装而言。 过渡的豪华的商品包装有可能会给社会及个人带来巨大的浪费，因此是不可以被鼓励的。

完美的商业活动需要完美的商业包装，然而商业的实质毕竟是商业，因此绝不可以**以噎废食**，以商业包装为理由来阻碍商业的发展，放弃商业机会。因此，完美的商业活动需要的其实是合适的商业包装。

Saturday, July 26, 2014

The Spirit and Definition of Business

[商业的精神及定义]

Today business activities have become increasingly frequent and the range of business activities has become increasingly wide, non-standardized and seemly standardized business practices have become more popular. In such situation, it is necessary to **remind ourselves of the spirit and the definition of business**, so we can serve our society with better business practices.

Business refers to providing services or products to customers in the market in exchange for others' services or products, or for exchangeable currencies. This is business. What is the spirit of business? **The spirit of business means favoring meeting the need of customers in the market with provided services or products as first priority, favoring the pursuit of profit and interest as second priority.** That is to say that in the business operation, we must first consider the needs of customers in the market and the services or products which can meet such needs, on this basis we can supplementally consider to increase earnings and profits. From the perspective of value, there are **two aspects of the concept of value regarding creating** value with business practice, **the value of the product** or service itself and **the added value** generated when the product or service is sold during the selling process (**added product value**). In terms of the priority, product value and added product value are just as important as each other.

However, looking at the reality of today's society, (business operated) only for profit, regardless of the real purpose of the services they provided, even sacrifice the needs of customers in the market. This phenomenon is particularly prominent in the internet industry. This business practice is really contrary to the spirit of business. **Customer first, service first, these are the eternal business rules.** Hopefully, every business can respect these business rules.

在当今商业活动日益频繁，活动范围日益广泛，不规范及貌似规范的商业行为越来越猖獗的形势下，我们很有必要**重温一下商业的精神及定义**，使我们的商业行为能够更好地服务于我们的社会。

商业，是指以自己的服务或产品提供给市场中的客户以换取对方的服务或产品或可用于交换的货币。这就是商业。商业的精神又是什么呢？**商业的精神是指以所提供的服务或产品满足市场中客户的需求为第一优先，以盈利及利润的追求为第二优先。**也就是说在商业的经营中，首先要考虑市场中客户的需求及满足此需求的服务或产品，在此基础之上辅之以考虑盈利及利润的增加。从价值的角度来讲，以商业的行为来创造价值，有**两个方面的价值的概念**：即产品或服务本身的**产品价值**和售出及售出过程中所产生的**附加价值（产品附加值**）。就优先权来讲，产品价值和产品附加值是一样重要的。

然而， 纵观当今的社会现实，只为盈利， 而不顾其所提供的服务的真正目的，甚至不惜牺牲市场用户的需求。这种现象在互联网行业尤为突出。这种商业行为实在是有悖于商业的精神。**用户至上，服务第一，这是永恒不变的商业规则。**但愿每一个商家都能够尊重这一商业规则。

Sunday, July 13, 2014

New Interventionism

[新干涉主义]

Today's world is increasingly integrated, information exchanges and communicates both quickly and widely, international trade makes relationships among countries more closely, international immigration makes relationships among peoples in different countries beyond the boundaries, this is the so-called global integration. In this situation, a country or an international organization conducts official or unofficial intervention on the internal events that occurred in another country in some degree is not surprising. The new interventionism is just developed in this environment.

For new interventionism, different countries, different

groups, awareness is different. For example speaking, there are advocates of human rights above sovereignty as new interventionism; there are advocates of bypassing international organizations or international laws as new interventionism. So, in the end what kind definition should be given to the new interventionism? **The new interventionism shall be the friendly, well-intentioned advocates and actions proposed or taken to help to maintain peace and order in the object country, and to help to promote the economic development of the object country while respecting for its national sovereignty and respecting for the rules of international laws.**

As progresses of economic and social development in different countries are different, the understandings of social development are different, often there will be **"those involved confused, those observed understood"** phenomenon, in this situation, the new interventionism will play the role of **taking thousand kilograms with one figure**, which will let people feel **stopper is removed suddenly**, thus narrowing the gap between social development   cognitions.

The new interventionism helps to improve the poor, uncultured internal management and event handling practice, thus promoting the pace of progress of human civilization   as   a   whole.

Of course, if the new interventionism surpassed the national sovereignty, surpassed the rules of international laws, it cannot be included in the scope of the new interventionism. New interventionism shall focus more on economic and social development, shall play its due role in promoting international economic cooperation and creating **international economic wheel**.

In respect of human rights, new interventionism has all the rights to criticize the incidents of human rights violations across the world. But in terms of military intervention, it cannot be called as new interventionism. **Military intervention belongs to the traditional interventionism** and is the last strategy of last resort. **Military intervention must act under the authority of the United Nations or regional international organizations.**

In short, the right new interventionism is a good medicine to help **the world's common development**.

当今的世界日益融合，信息的沟通与交流既迅速又广泛，国际贸易使得国与国之间的关系越发紧密，国际移民使得不同国家人民之间的关系超越了国界的限制，这也就是所谓的**全球一体化**。在这种形势下，一个国家或国际组织对另外一个国家所发生的内部事件进行官方的或民间的程度不同的干预也就不足为奇了。新干涉主义正是在这种环境下产生的。

对于新干涉主义，不同的国家，不同的集团，认识是不同的。举例讲，有主张人权高于主权的新干涉主义；有主张超越国际组织或国际法的新干涉主义。那么，到底应当给与新干涉主义什么样的定义呢？新干涉主义应当是在尊重国家主权，尊重国际法准则的前提下，对对象国友好的，善意的，有助于维护对象国的和平与秩序，有助于推动对象国的经济发展的主张和行动。

由于不同国家经济和社会发展的进度不同，对社会发展的认识不同，时常会出现"当事者迷，旁观者清"的现象，在这种情况下，新干涉主义就会起到一两拨千斤的作用，使人茅塞顿开，从而缩小对社会发展认知的差距。

新干涉主义有助于校正不良的，落后的内部管理和事件处理方式，从而推动人类文明整体前进的步伐。

当然，新干涉主义如果超越了国家主权，超越了国际法准则，就不可以归入新干涉主义的范畴。新干涉主义更应当着重于经济和社会发展方面，要为国际经济协作，造就国际经济轮而发挥应有的作用。

就人权而言，新干涉主义对发生在世界范围内的践踏人权的事件，都有抨击的权利，但就军事干涉而言，则不能够称之为新干涉主义。军事干涉属于传统的干涉主义，是万不得已的最后策略。军事干涉一定要在联合国或地区国际组织的授权下行动。

总之，正确的新干涉主义是有助于世界共同发展的一剂良药。

Sunday, July 6, 2014

Learning Capability, Innovation Capability, Teaching Capability

[学习的能力，创新的能力，传授的能力]

Having the capability to **learn** is not surprising, having the capability of **innovation** and the capability to **teach**, can only mean to have the perfect personality for a man , and so for a nation.

有**学习**的能力，不足为奇，有**创新**的能力，并有**传授**的能力，才为有**完美的人格**，对于一个人是如此，对于一个民族也是一样的。

Sunday, June 15, 2014

Politics - Country Management - Foreign Relation - Guiding Principles for Foreign Aid Work Under New Situation

[政治 - 国家管理 - 外交关系 - 新形势下的外援工作指导原则]

Foreign aid work is a very important task in a country's foreign relation development, especially for developed countries and big countries. History of foreign aid is also long-standing, and the focus of each country's foreign aid work is not the same in different historic periods. So in current new situation, what kind **guiding principles** shall we have for **the foreign aid work**?

Surely someone will ask, what is **the current new situation?** In fact, we are well aware, the tide of the **internationalization** promoted by the IT technology is surging, the situation of **debt crisis in Europe** is still serious, **United States has more debts** after the financial crisis, only **BRICS countries** (Brazil, Russia, India, China, South Africa) have strong economic growth, but most of them have large population and weak infrastructure. **Economic globalization** makes more interdependence of more countries' economies; the characteristics of **economic wheel** become increasingly evident.

Thus, **foreign aid work shall have the following guiding principles under the new situation:**

1. **Foreign aid work shall add bricks and tiles for the economic recovery, and make due contributions to the construction of regional or international economic wheel;**

2. **Foreign aid work, shall be extremely elegant and valuable, shall let the people of the recipient country really feel the love of the people from the aiding country, shall have the thinking of fame and fortune, shall be glorifying to remember aid work figures in history;**

3. **Foreign aid work, particularly in the international humanitarian aid, shall strive to eliminate the root causes of generating international refugees; while aiding international refugees, the interests of underdeveloped areas shall be considered;**

4. Foreign aid work, shall balance the political, security and economic factors, and try to achieve the objectives of the trinity as far as possible.

Of course, foreign aid work involves more aspects, such as forms of assistance and so on. I will not talk more specific here.

对外援助，在一个国家的对外交往中，是一个非常重要的工作，尤其是对于发达国家和大国来讲。对外援助的历史也由来以久，而在历史的各个不同时期，各个国家的对外援助工作的重点也是不一样的。那么在当前的新形势下，**对外援助的工作**应当具有什么样的**指导原则**呢？

一定有人会问，**当前的新形势**又是什么样的呢？其实大家都很清楚，在 IT 技术推动下的**国际化**大潮涌动，**欧洲债务危机**形势依然严重，**美国**在金融危机后更是**债台高筑**，只有**金砖国家**（巴西，俄罗斯，印度，中国，南非）经济增长势头强劲，但他们大多人口众多，基础设施薄弱。**经济全球化**使得更多国家的经济更加相互依存；**经济轮**特征日益明显。

因此，**新形势下的对外援助的工作**应当具有以下的指导原则：

1。 对外援助的工作要为经济复苏增砖添瓦，要为地区或国际性的经济轮的建设做出应有的贡献；

2。 对外援助工作，要掷地有声，要让受援国的人民真正感受到援助国人民的情和意，要有名利的思想，要树碑立传，要在历史中留下援助者的身影；

3。 对外援助工作，尤其是在国际人道主义援助，要努力消除国际难民产生的根源； 在援助国际难民的同时，要考虑不发达地区的利益；

4。 对外援助工作，政治，安全和经济的因素要统筹兼顾，要尽可能的实现三位一体的目标；

当然，对外援助工作涉及到更多的方面，例如，援助形式，等等。我这里就不再谈更具体的了。

Saturday, June 7, 2014

Time to Reach a Final Deal - On the Relationship of Israel and Palestine

[达成最终协议的时机已到 - 论以色列和巴勒斯坦的关系]

In the international political arena, **the Israelis and Palestinians** are the most on the stage. Since **<<Resolution 181>>** of the United Nations agreed in November 1947, wars and conflicts between Israel and Palestine had never been stopped, the peace talks between Israel and Palestine had also been engaged in intermittent. From the **<<Camp David Accords>>** signed in 1978 in Carter era to the **<<Madrid Peace Framework>>** agreed in 1991 in the Senior Bush era; from the **<<Oslo Agreement>>** signed in 1993 in Clinton era to the **<<Sharm El-Sheikh Memo>>** agreed in 2000; from the **<<Middle East Peace Plan>>** drafted in 2002 in Junior Bush era to the most recent **<<Obama's Advocates>>** in 2011, thirty six years have passed, the peace agreement between Israel and Palestine has not yet been settled. It is time for us to make further efforts to reach a final agreement.

In my opinion, the normal relation between Israel and Palestine should first follow the following basic principles:

Each shall mutually recognize and respect the others' right to survival;

Each shall mutually recognize and respect the others' right to development;

To encourage and promote common development concept;

To encourage and promote common security concept;

Israelis and Palestinians shall regard each other as their own brothers. That is like what is said in the Bible, <<Romans>> Chapter 12 Section 10: "**love brothers, Affectionate to one another; respect person, be modesty to one another.**" They shall have the verve of **universal brotherhood** as preached by the Islam. If each other can give a step out to the others, things can be solved more easily.

To solve issue of the Israeli-Palestinian relation, I think that **the Independent and Cooperated new model** can be taken to deal with it, such as: Jerusalem, security, water resource and so on. Palestine shall become an independent state; Israel shall withdraw from all occupied territories. Jerusalem can be a shared capital and can be jointly managed as a special district. Security and water resource all can be managed with joint management model, because after all, it comes to the survival of two nations. If there is sovereignty issue involved in the joint management model, it can take **the separation of sovereignty and management right model** to deal with. Refugee return issue can take the principle of voluntary returns, the possible workload and instability should be minimized.

For the development issue of Israel and Palestine, it can take **multi-layer structure** to deal with, such as: establishing **the Cooperation Council** between the independent Israel and Palestinian states; establishing **economic union** with more inter-regional countries. Israel shall take the leader role to play in the regional economic development. Israel and neighboring countries in the region shall establish "**building a better home together**" theme willing, and make due contributions for regional economic development and improving people's lives.

There are **one and one pearls inlaid in Eastern Arabian**

Peninsula, why has Northern Arabian Peninsula lost its luster? I hope that Israel and Palestine can turn out to be **the North Stars of the Arabian Peninsula** after peace making.

在国际政治舞台上，登台演出最多的莫过于**以色列人和巴勒斯坦人**了。自 1947 年 11 月联合国达成<<**181 号决议**>>以来，以巴之间的战争和冲突就没有停止过，以巴之间的和平谈判也一直在断断续续地进行着。从 1978 年卡特时期的<<**戴维营协议**>>到 1991 年老布什时期的<<**马德里和平框架**>>；从 1993 年克林顿时期的<<**奥斯陆协议**>>到 2000 年的<<**沙姆沙伊赫备忘录**>>；从 2002 年小布什时期的<<**中东和平计划**>>到最近的 2011 年的<<**奥巴马主张**>>，三十六年过去了，以巴之间的和平协议还没有尘埃落定。是我们应该做出进一步努力，达成最终协议的时候了。

在我看来，正常的以色列和巴勒斯坦的关系首先应当遵循以下几项基本原则：

要各自互相承认和尊重对方的生存权；

要各自互相承认和尊重对方的发展权；

要鼓励和倡导共同发展观；

要鼓励和倡导共同安全观；

以色列人和巴勒斯坦人要各自视对方为自己的兄弟。要像圣经《罗马书》12 章 10 节说的那样：**"爱弟兄，要彼此亲热；恭敬人，要彼此推让"**。要有伊斯兰所宣扬的四海皆兄弟的气魄。如果彼此各让一步，事情就容易解决的多。

解决以巴关系的问题，我认为可以采取**独立加合作的新模式**来处理，例如：耶路撒冷，安全，水资源等。巴勒斯坦应该成为一个独立国家，以色列应该撤出所有被占领土。耶路撒冷可以是共有的首都，可以采取特区的模式共同管理。安全和水资源均可采取共同管理的模式进行管理，因为毕竟涉及到两个民族的生存问题。在共同管理中涉及主权的议题，可以采取**主权与管理权分离的模式**来处理。难民回归的问题可以采取自愿回归的原则，应尽量减少可能增加的工作量及不稳定因素。

对于以色列和巴勒斯坦的发展问题，可以采取**多层结构**来处理，例如：在独立的以色列和巴勒斯坦国之间建立**合作委员会**；在更多的地区国家间建立**经济联盟**。以色列在地区经济发展中应当起到带头的作用。以色列和周边地区国家应该确立"**共建美好家园**"主题意愿，要确确实实的为发展地区经济，改善人民生活做出应有的贡献。

阿拉伯半岛的东方镶嵌着**一颗又一颗明珠**，为什么阿拉伯半岛的北方却暗淡无光？ 但愿和平后的以色列和巴勒斯坦能够成为阿拉伯半岛的**北方之星**。

Sunday, June 1, 2014

52

<<Bird View>>

United Asia - Asia Security Council –
The Future of Asia's Security Structure

[联合的亚洲 - 亚洲安全理事会 - 亚洲安全结构的未来]

Asia security issue is not only an issue concerned by the people of Asia, but also an issue concerned by the people around the world. Why? Because of a series of security-related events that occurred over the years in Asia, which not only bring a profound impact on the life of the people of Asia, but also bring a shocking impact on the life of the people around the world, such as: **multiple wars in Afghanistan, Iran-Iraq war, the war in Kuwait, multiple wars in Iraq, the war between China and Vietnam, the recent turmoils in the Arab spring, the civil war in Syria**

and **the unrest replacements of the Egyptian government, and so on.**

The reasons for these events, or are because of so-called the presence of terrorists in Asia, or are because of the territorial disputes, or are because of competing interests and rights. No matter for whatever reasons, all have described **the presence of the security issues inside Asia,** and these security issues have not been handled well at the international level (United Nations or current regional organizations), it is stated that **there are problems in the mechanism to deal with the problem of security issues in Asia.**

So how to better improve the mechanism for dealing with Asia security problems? As stated in my article <<Politics - Country Management - UN & Regional International Organizations [政治 - 国家管理 - 联合国和地区国际组织]>> advocated strengthening the construction of regional international organizations, establishing a United **Asian Union,** I advocate to establish **regional security institutions** based on the establishment of **regional international organizations,** namely the **Asia Security Council.** So we can strive to have Asia's security issues to be solved inside Asia first by Asians.

Establishing Asia Security Council, comparing with the existing mechanism, can eliminate the following errors when dealing the security issues:

- United Asia Security Council can eliminate the East-West confrontation color;
- United Asia Security Council can eliminate the religious confrontation color;
- United Asia Security Council can eliminate the colonialism and anti-colonialism confrontation color;
- United Asia Security Council can eliminate the ideological confrontation color;
- United Asia Security Council can eliminate the developed and underdeveloped country confrontation color;
- United Asia Security Council can eliminate the racial confrontation color;
- United Asia Security Council can remove the Allies and the Axis confrontation color under the shadow of World War II;
- United Asia Security Council can eliminate the industrial and non-industrial countries confrontation colors;
- United Asia Security Council can eliminate the large countries and country groups confrontation color;
- United Asia Security Council can eliminate the confrontation color caused by the historical grievances;

Based on this, the security problems in Asia could be the internal problems in Asia to the most, to be solved by Asians within Asia to the greatest extent possible, thus reducing the negative impacts on their own and the world brought by the security issues in Asia to the maximum extent possible.

The world needs to go forward, the world security structure needs to be improved, improving the security structure in Asia bears the brunt. **United Asia, the united Asia Security Council under the leadership of United Asian Union is bound to be the future of Asia's security structure.**

亚洲的安全，不仅是亚洲人民所关注的议题，也是全世界人民所关注的议题。为什么？ 因为这些年来在亚洲所发生的一系列与安全相关的事件，不仅给亚洲人民的生活带来深远的影响，更给全世界人民的生活带来震撼性的影响，例如：**多次的阿富汗战争，两伊战争，科威特之战，多次的伊拉克战争，中越之战，最近的动荡的阿拉伯之春，叙利亚内战以及动荡的埃及政府的更换,**等等。

这些事件的原因或因为所谓的亚洲区存在恐怖分子，或因为领土之争，或因为利益及权利之争，但无论是何种原因，都说明**亚洲区内部存在安全的问题**，而这些安全问题在国际层面上（联合国或现存的地区国际组织）没有得到较好地处理，更说明**处理亚洲安全问题的机制存在一定的问题。**

那么如何更好的完善处理亚洲安全问题的机制呢？同我在上一篇文章《Politics - Country Management - UN & Regional International Organizations [政治 - 国家管理 - 联合国和地区国际组织]》所主张的加强地区性国际组织的建设，建立统一的**亚洲联盟**一样，我主张在建立**地区性国际组织**的基础之上，建立**地区性安全机构**，也就是**亚洲安全理事会**。这样就可以争取使亚洲的安全问题首先在亚洲内部由亚洲人来解决。

建立亚洲安全理事会，同现行方式相比，可以消除以下几种解决安全问题的误差：

- 统一的亚洲安全理事会可以消除东西方对抗的色彩；
- 统一的亚洲安全理事会可以消除宗教对抗的色彩；
- 统一的亚洲安全理事会可以消除殖民主义和反殖民主义对抗的色彩；
- 统一的亚洲安全理事会可以消除意识形态对抗的色彩；
- 统一的亚洲安全理事会可以消除发达与不发达国家对抗的色彩；
- 统一的亚洲安全理事会可以消除种族对抗的色彩；
- 统一的亚洲安全理事会可以消除二战阴影下，轴心国和同盟国对抗的色彩；
- 统一的亚洲安全理事会可以消除工业国家和非工业国家对抗的色彩；
- 统一的亚洲安全理事会可以消除大国与大国集团对抗的色彩；
- 统一的亚洲安全理事会可以消除因历史恩怨而对抗的色彩；

基于此，亚洲的安全问题就可以尽最大可能的成为亚洲内部的问题，尽最大可能的由亚洲人在亚洲内部自行解决，从而尽最大可能的减少亚洲的安全问题给自己及世界所带来的负面的影响。

世界要发展，世界的安全结构要完善，亚洲安全结构的完善是首当其冲的。**联合的亚洲，在亚洲联盟主持下的统一的亚洲安全理事会必将是亚洲安全结构的未来。**

Sunday, May 25, 2014

Politics - Country Management - UN & Regional International Organizations

[政治 - 国家管理 - 联合国和地区国际组织]

In today's international relation management and international conflict management, the United Nations plays a decisive crucial role. The United Nations is an international organization composed of sovereign states after World War II, the "UN Charter" signed in force in **San Francisco** on **October 24, 1945** marks the formal establishment of the United Nations. The United Nations currently has **193 member states**.

Since its establishment, the United Nations has made an outstanding contribution for the maintenance of world peace, relaxing international tensions and resolving regional conflicts, promoting economic, scientific and cultural cooperation and exchanges among member states. For example: **the maintenance of peace and observer missions** sent by the United Nations, the United Nations **Millennium Development Goals Project, UNICEF** of the United Nations, '**Universal Declaration of Human Rights**' adopted by the UN General Assembly, the "**United Nations Framework Convention on Climate Change**" in negotiation, and so on.

However, in a simple majority voting mechanism, due to **regional differences** and **cognitive differences on the target countries** for the resolution, in some cases, a resolution with certain deviations from the fact may arise. On the other hand, due to **economic and financial reasons**, the deviations brought by large countries and influential power country groups to the resolutions and actions can not be ignored. In another aspect, some member states act beyond the jurisdiction of the United Nations, and bring **misleading deviations in public opinion** on UN resolutions and actions. These are the problems that the United Nations currently has.

So, if we can **strengthen the role of regional international organization** while **strengthening the leadership role of the United Nations**, these deviations will be greatly reduced. Regional international organization has a better understanding of the local affairs, a more close relationship, can handle the local affairs more effectively, and will avoid major big mistakes. Regional international organization like the computer's **buffer**, if functioning well, it will greatly **improve the efficiency of international management, reduce risks and errors, improve financial conditions**, so that the existing international management system can be improved further.

Currently, the regional international organizations like the United Nations are: the **European Union, the African Union, the Organization of American States**, and so on. Asia has a lot of international organizations, such as: Commonwealth of Independent States, the Shanghai Cooperation Organization, ASEAN, APEC, the Gulf Arab States Cooperation Committee, and so on. But most of them emphasize on economic cooperation. Seen this in light, to establish a united **Asian Union** is an important step to improve the existing international management system. This is also an important part of the Asia security strategy. As for Oceania, due to its geographical location and economic relation, or it can be incorporated into the Asian Union, or it can establish an independent **Oceania Union**.

In short, the United Nations' leadership should be strengthened, while, the regional international organizations likes the United Nations should be improved further, which is the key to improve the efficiency of international management, to reduce risks and errors.

在当今的国际关系管理和国际冲突管理中，联合国发挥着决定性的至关重要的作用。联合国是在第二次世界大战后由主权国家组成的国际组织，**1945 年 10 月 24 日**在美国旧金山签署生效的《联合国宪章》标志着联合国的正式成立。联合国目前共有**193 个成员国**。

联合国自成立以来，为维护世界和平，缓和国际紧张局势，解决地区冲突，促进成员国之间的经济，科学，文化合作与交流做出了卓越的贡献。例如：联合国派出的**维持和平特派团和观察团**，联合国的**千年发展目标项目**，联合国的**儿童基金会**，联合国大会通过的《世界人权宣言》，磋商中的《联合国气候变化框架公约》，等等。

然而，在以简单多数的投票机制中，由于**地区的差异性**及对决议**对象国认知的差异性**，在某些情况下，就有可能产生于事实有一定偏差的决议。另外一方面，由于**经济和金融的原因**，大国和大国集团的影响力所带来的决议和行为偏差也是不可忽视的。再一方面，某些成员国超越联合国的管辖，**在舆论上为联合国的决议和行为带来误导性偏差**。 这就是联合国现在所存在的问题。

那么，如果能够在**加强联合国领导作用**的同时，**加强地区性国际组织的作用**，这些偏差就会大大减少。地区性国际组织对本地区的事务更了解，关系更紧密，对事务的处理可能会更有效，同时可以避免重大的失误。地区性国际组织就好像计算机的**缓存器**，如果运作良好，就会大大**提高国际管理的效率，降低风险和失误，改进财务状况**，从而使得现有的国际管理体系得到进一步的完善。

目前，类似于联合国的地区性国际组织有：**欧洲联盟，非洲联盟，美洲国家组织**，等等。亚洲有很多国际组织，例如：独立国家联合体，上海合作组织，东南亚国家联盟，亚太经济合作组织，海湾阿拉伯国家合作委员会，等等。但大多偏重于经济合作。由此看来，建立统一的**亚洲联盟**是完善现有国际管理体系的重要一步。这也是亚洲安全策略的重要一环。至于大洋洲，由于其地理位置和经济关系的原因，或可并入亚洲联盟，或可成立独立的**大洋洲联盟**。

总之，联合国的领导地位要加强，同时要进一步完善类似于联合国的地区性国际组织，这是提高国际管理的效率，降低风险和失误的关键所在。

Saturday, May 17, 2014

Freedom World, Freedom Air - Bentham's Doctrine and Modern Legislative System

[自由的世界，自由的空气 - 边沁学说与现代立法制度]

Jeremy Bentham's utilitarian philosophy of legislation is the spiritual cornerstone of modern British government system. Modern parliamentary legislative system is built on the principles of utilitarian and the maximum happiness principle advocated by Jeremy Bentham. In my previous article, "political opportunism and political utilitarianism", I have given a summary definition of political utilitarianism, **which refers to using the government's rights to influence and pursue common interests of all members of society on political morality, which is referred to the greatest happiness and joys of individual members of society on moral utilitarianism.**

Today after experiencing hundreds of years of utilitarian legislation, shall we have a deep reflection? Have a reflection in accordance with the principle of the maximum happiness advocated by Bentham? Have all of our government's legislative acts really met the common interests of all community members, ensured the maximum happiness and joys of all members of our society?

In my opinion, some of our legislative works are contrary to Bentham's principles of the maximum happiness. For example, **the provisions relating to the minutiae of everyday life, regulations cannot be fully complied by most people (including legislators), certain provisions brought by political frictions**, and so on.

Today, most works of the government management are achieved in the form of legislation. However, legal constraints for all members of society have two side effects, namely assurance role and the role of constraints, which are contradictory duality of opposites. For the management of individuals in a society, there shall be tightness with laxation. So I advocate two forms of legislation - **Binding Legislation and Guiding Legislation.**

The reason I put forward the **guiding legislation**, in fact, is a concrete manifestation of **flexible management** proposed by Bentham. Each sound educated individual in society has self-awareness, self-management capabilities. The distinction between legislative guidance apart will allow our legislative work more hierarchical. So each individual member of our society can feel the happiness and joy of self-management, thereby reducing the injuries and assaults to the individual member of society brought by the legislation and government management.

In short, society is going to develop, we are going to move forward, **the legislation is no exception**.

杰里米边沁的功利主义立法哲学是英国现代政体的精神基石。现代议会立法制度正是建立在杰里米边沁所提倡的功利原理和最大幸福原理之上的。在我前文《政治投机和政治功利主义》中，我曾给出政治功利主义的总结定义，即**政治功利主义是指政治道德上主张以政府的权利来影响和追求全体社会成员的普遍利益，也就是道德功利主义上所指的社会成员个体的最大的幸福和快乐。**

在经历了几百年的功利主义立法之后的今天，我们是不是有必要进行深入的反思？ 按照边沁所提倡的最大幸福原则进行反思？我们政府所有的立法行为是不是真正地满足了全体社会成员的普遍利益，并保证了全体社会成员个体的最大的幸福和快乐呢？

在我看来，有些立法工作是与边沁的最大幸福原则相违背的。例如，有关日常生活中的细枝末节的规定，有关大多数人（包括立法者）都无法完全守约的规定，某些属于政治内耗的规定，等等。

当今，政府管理大多数是以立法的形式来实现的。然而，法律的约束对于全体社会成员是具有两面作用的，即保证的作用和约束的作用，这就是对立矛盾的双重性。对于社会个体的管理，要张而有驰。因此我主张两种形式的立法 -- **约束性立法和指导性立法**。

我之所以提出**指导性立法**，其实也就是边沁所提出的**柔性管理**的具体体现。每一个健全的受过教育的社会个体都有自我认知，自我管理的能力。将指导性立法区别开来，这样可以使我们的立法工作更有层次性。使我们社会的每一个个体成员都能够感受到自我管理的幸福和快乐，从而减少立法和政府管理工作本身对社会个体成员所带来的伤害与侵犯。

总之，社会是要发展的，我们都是要前行的，**立法工作也不例外**。

Sunday, May 4, 2014

Religion - We Are the Same

[宗教- 我们是相同的]

In this world, almost no one country or region can not be affected by religion, whether Christianity, Islam or Buddhism, and so on. The impact of religion on the world can be described as obvious, universally acknowledged. It is so because we human beings' knowledge on the world and we human beings' cognitive ability to the world are limited. This world has too many things we human beings can not control, can not predict or can not recognize, so a spiritual sustenance is needed, an idol as a spiritual existence beyond the ability of human beings is needed. Almost all religions have their own idol, so all religions are the same, the differences are the external manifestation and the distance with **Datong society**, and so on.

From another perspective, all religions have a standard as the code of conduct to deal with others, have an aspect of education for personal growth. For example: Christianity advocates fraternity, equality before God; Christianity advocates inclusive, progressive spirit, admiration and gratitude for Jesus Christ; Christianity advocates freedom, democracy, righteousness, loyalty and moral; Christianity advocates eliminating bad desires in heart, practicing repentance for their own mistakes and committed sins, purifying their minds.

Islam advocates obedience and faith in Allah, the only and highest Dominate in the universe, in order to achieve two world peace and tranquility. Islam advocates a comprehensive peace and unity with particular emphasizing on education and questing for knowledge. Islam considers: the entire history of human beings is that Allah sent messengers to teach human beings to know **Tawheed**, a process to promote good and curb evils in the process, the mission of angels and prophets of each successive dynasties are in the same strain.

Buddhism may be more than an exception, because there is not an all-powerful Buddhist idol. Buddhism believes that everyone's fate rests in his own hands. Buddhism advocates self-life care. Because whether we repay our parents up bringing, pursuit happy life in the world, or practice Dharma, pursuit the interests of the free world, all must rely on our extremely rare precious personal lives.

On their relations, Islam and Christianity are all belong to Abraham Department. Christianity believes that Jesus is the Son of God, Islam only think that Jesus is a prophet holding the same position as Abraham, Moses and Mohammed. God picks a prophet every time, and bestowed by volume, but Muhammad was "seal the Holy of Holies.", the last prophet selected by God.

Religion is the same, especially for saying of Islam and Christianity.

在这个世界上，几乎没有一个国家或地区能够不受宗教的影响的，无论是基督教，伊斯兰教或佛教，等等。宗教对于世界的影响之大，可谓是有目共睹，举世公认。其之所以如此，是因为我们人类对于世界的认知和我们人类自身的能力是有限的。这个世界有太多人类无法控制，无法预知或无法认知的事情，因此需要一个精神上的寄托，一个精神上存在的，能力上超越众生的偶像。几乎所有的宗教都有自己的偶像，因此，所有的宗教其实是一样的，所不同的就是外在的表现，与大同社会距离的远近，等等。

从另外一个角度讲，所有的宗教都有规范为人处事行为准则的内涵，对于个人成长都有教育的一个方面。例如：基督教主张博爱，在上帝面前人人平等；基督教提倡包容、进步精神，敬仰并感恩基督；基督教号召自由、民主、仁义、义气与道义；基督教主张消除内心的不良欲望，对犯下的过错和自身的罪恶进行忏悔，净化心灵。

伊斯兰教主张顺从和信仰宇宙独一的最高主宰安拉及其意志，以求得两世的和平与安宁。伊斯兰教主张全面和平和团结，伊斯兰教特别强调教育和求知。伊斯兰教认为：人类整个历史是真主派遣使者教导人类认主独一，扬善制恶的过程，历代众使者和先知的使命是一脉相承的。

佛教可能是比较例外的，因为佛教里没有一个全能的偶像。佛教相信每个人的命运都掌握在自己手中。佛教主张爱惜自我的生命。因为无论我们报答父母的养育之恩，追求世间的幸福生活，还是修学佛法，追求出世间的解脱利益，都要依靠这极为难得的宝贵人身。

就他们的关系而言，伊斯兰教和基督教同属亚伯拉罕系。基督教相信耶稣为上帝的儿子，伊斯兰教认为耶稣只为先知，与亚伯拉罕、摩西和穆罕默德持同样地位，上帝每隔一段时间要挑选一位先知，并赐予经卷，但穆罕默德为"封印至圣"，即上帝挑选的最后一位先知。

宗教是相同的，尤其是对于伊斯兰教和基督教而言。

[Reference1: http://baike.baidu.com/view/916005.htm]
[Reference 2: http://baike.baidu.com/view/8241.htm]
[Reference 3: http://baike.baidu.com/view/9414.htm]
[Reference 4: http://baike.baidu.com/view/4696.htm]

Sunday, April 20, 2014

On Leadership

[论领导力]

In all countries,
I need leader to lead all nations,
Not just your own nation.

In the world,
I need leader to lead all countries,
Not just your own country.

在所有国家，
我需要领导者去引领所有的民族，
不只是你自己的民族。

在世界上，
我需要领导者去引领所有的国家，
不只是你自己的国家。

Sunday, April 20, 2014

Politics - Party - How to Build Up Normal and Reasonable Exit Mechanism

[政治 - 政党 - 如何建立正常的理性的退出机制]

In modern multi-party election system, the ruling party can win the election from the intense competition, is not an easy thing. An elected member, of course, will show glories on face and complaisant in determination after being elected. After a period of orientation and training, he gradually gets into the role and began to unleash his own leadership and coordination in community and government management operations. However, any level of government is not once and for all, **not for a lifetime**. Therefore, **how to establish a normal and reasonable exit mechanism to avoid expendable exit** is particularly important.

In modern multi-party election system, the ruling party can not always maintain its position as a ruling party has its own underlying causes. **The first** is that the election cycle determines the ruling party must face the voters' test every few years; **secondly**, the ruling party's performance may have more or less distances between voters' expectation; **the third**, development direction of the domestic affairs or constituency may require some adjustments after a period of time; **the fourth**, international affairs or government relations may also require some adjustments after a period of time; **the fifth,** elected member may need to adjust his own personal life direction after experiencing certain terms; **the sixth**, elected member lacks the re-election intrinsic motivation due to the generous retirement benefits after experiencing certain terms.

So, then, how to establish normal and reasonable exit mechanism to avoid expendable exit? The so-called **expendable exit** means to seek some external excuses for exit, for example: events, wrong decisions or improper behaviors and so on. Expendable exist will bring some negative effects to the voters, the constituency or the country or himself. **Normal and reasonable exit mechanism** actually refers to **the voluntary withdrawal mechanism without any reason**.

Of course, related parties or professionals may have better ideas to establish a normal and reasonable exit mechanism, then I would applaud for it. In short, we should try to avoid and reduce internal frictions and negative things, and try to make our society much better!

在现代多党选举体制中，执政党能够从激烈的选举中胜出，实在不是一件容易的事情。一个议员在当选后当然是荣光焕发，踌躇满志，在经过一段时期的锤炼后，也逐渐步入角色。在社区和政府的管理运作中，开始发挥自己的领导与协调的作用。然而，任何一级的政府都不是一劳永逸的，都不**是终身的**。因此，如何**建立正常的理性的退出机制，避免消耗性的退出**，就显得格外重要。

在现代多党选举体制中，一个执政党不可能永远保持执政党的地位是有其**内在原因**的。**首先**是选举周期决定了执政党每隔几年都要面临选民的考验；**其次**，执政党的表现可能与选民的期望有或多或少的距离；**第三**，国内事务或选区的发展方向可能在经过一段时间后需要一定的调整；**第四**，国际事务或政府关系可能在经过一段时间后也需要一定的调整；**第五**，当选议员个人在经历一定的任期后，其个人人生的发展方向面临调整；**第六**，当选议员个人在经历一定的任期后，由于优厚的退休待遇使其缺乏竞选连任的内在动力。

既然如此，那么，如何建立正常的理性的退出机制，避免消耗性的退出呢？所谓**消耗性退出**，是指寻求一定的外在借口，例如：事件，错误的决定或不当的行为，等等。消耗性退出是会给选民，选区或国家及本人带来一定的负面效应的。**正常的理性的退出机制其实就是指自愿性的无理由退出机制**。

当然，也许有关方面或专业人士对于建立正常的理性的退出机制有更好的主张，那我将鼓掌欢迎。总之，我们应当尽量避免和减少内耗和负面的东西，使我们的社会更美好！

Saturday, April 12, 2014

The Mettle of Indian

[印度人的气概]

As I write this article, the Indians have started to construct the world's tallest statue - **Statue of Unity** on **January 26** this year (2014). The statue is to commemorate the founding father of India - **Sardar. Patel**. According to reports, this statue is 182 meters high, which is twice as that of the U.S. Statue of Liberty, and five times as that of the Redeemer in Rio De Janeiro in Brazil. What a grand statue! Ah! He will become another remarkable magnificent landscape place in the world. It also shows the mettle of Indians to be **reborn**, to **transform themselves** to become a pointing at the sky independent country in the world.

India this country has inextricably links with China in history, but not tight. Buddhism which came to China from India had a more profound impact on China. As the mountain barrier, the communion between Chinese people and Indians in history is extremely inconvenient. From the point of view of safety, either from historical view, or from realistic view, the external conditions for China and India to threat each other do not exist.

From the point of view of national development, China and India have many similarities, such as: **population issue**, **environment issue**, **resource issue**, and **education issue**, etc. In my view, in order to achieve the development for the India's rebirth, it has to take the **learning and innovation** two roads **simultaneously. National Education** is perhaps the first one. Increasing **the living standard of people**, so the society can have a whole new look.

In conclusion, I wish that Indians can transform the rebirth mettle to courage and wisdom in reality, so as to achieve the dream of self- transformation!

在我写这篇文章的时候，印度人已经于今年（2014）一月二十六号开始动工兴建这座世界上最高的**联合雕像**了。这座雕像是为纪念印度立国的开国元勋**萨德尔.帕特尔**的。据介绍，这座雕像高 182 米，是美国自由女神像的两倍，是巴西里约热内卢救世主像的 5 倍。这是一个多么宏大的雕像啊，他必将成为世界上又一处令人瞩目的宏伟景观。这也显示出印度人决心**脱胎换骨**，改造**自我**，成为世界上顶天立地独立国家的气概。

<<Bird View>>

印度这个国家在历史上同中国有着千丝万缕的联系，但并不紧密。从印度传入中国的佛教却对中国产生了较为深远的影响。由于高山的阻隔，中国人和印度人在历史上的交往是极不便利的。从安全的角度来说，无论从历史上来看，还是从现实来看，中国和印度相互威胁的外在条件是不具备的。

从国家发展来看，中国和印度有着许多相似的地方，例如：**人口问题，环境问题，资源问题**，以及**教育问题**，等等。以我来看，印度要想取得脱胎换骨的发展，就要走**借鉴与独创**并举的道路。**国民教育**也许是第一位的。同时提高**人民安居生活的标准**，从而使整个社会焕然一新。

总之，我祝愿印度人能够化脱胎换骨的气概为现实中的勇气和智慧，从而实现改造自我的梦想！

Saturday, March 29, 2014

Politics - Society - Democracy - Democratic Right & Protest Demonstration

[政治- 社会 – 民主- 民主的权力和示威游行]

Protest Demonstration can be described as a common occurrence, easy to see event in many countries' political life. This is also a typical outward manifestation of **people's democratic right**. However, based on my observation, the demonstration is very easy to become a means for social unrest, a means for overthrowing the normal legal system, which is a **miracle circle** of modern democracy: **The voter based legislative system and the voter based demonstration to overthrow the legal system.**

Looking around the world, from **the Arab Spring** to **the European Debt Crisis,** from all over the world's **Occupation Movement** to **the Syria Crisis,** every major social event, all are closely related with voter based demonstrations. The results of such events not only bring disastrous consequences to the happened countries, but also bring an unbearable burden to the international community. So, how to treat such problems in the end? How to deal with them?

In fact, speaking from the theory of **political science** and **management science,** this is **a subject of voters' wish expression and expression management.** So, how to get voters to express their wishes correctly? How to manage the manner of voters' wish expression? Here I would like to state my view on demonstration, such a wish expression method:

Democratic right of demonstration can be said to have a long history, which is characterized by **massive, broad participation** and **influential.** However, in terms of wishes to express, not every participant knows his own wishes to express or the group's wishes to express. Therefore, the correct approach is: every demonstration should have **the wishes to express in written (petition),** should have **the served object (government, legislature** or **other relevant bodies),** the wishes to express shall be public appropriately.

An appropriate response shall be given by the served body within a certain period of time. Meanwhile, every demonstration shall have its organizers and schedules be opened in the public media. This can be **a mutual restraint mechanism**, so that voters can enjoy their democratic rights more rationally.

On the other hand, demonstration could not be continued without restraints, otherwise it is an abuse of democratic right, it is a damage to other voters' democratic rights. And therefore demonstration time should be limited, illustratively **one week, two weeks**, etc. This can make the greatest possible reduction of the negative impact that the demonstration may bring.

Of course, if there is **a mechanism of international participation**, pressure can be applied to the power politics or problem government, it would be a better choice, but there will be a suspicion of interference in the internal affairs.

In short, it should be improved for the demonstration as a wish expression manner; the managing style should also be improved. Therefore the social unrest and international burdens which demonstration may bring can be reduced. Hope my propositions can achieve extensive support and advocacy from the **Arab Countries**, the **European Countries** and other countries suffering hardship with demonstrations.

示威游行在许多国家的政治生活中，可谓是司空见惯，屡见不鲜。这也是人民**民主权利**的一种典型的，直接的外在表现。然而，基于本人的观察，示威游行却很容易成为社会动荡，成为一种推翻正常法律制度的手段，这也就是现代民主制度的一个**怪圈**： 基于选民的立法制度与以基于选民的示威游行推翻法律的制度。

放眼全球，从**阿拉伯之春**到**欧洲债务危机**，从遍布全球的**占领运动**到**叙利亚危机**，每一次的重大社会事件，无不和选民的示威游行紧密相关。这些事件的结果不仅给发生地国家带来灾难性的后果，也给国际社会带来难以承受的负担。那么，这个问题到底应当如何看待，如何处理呢？

其实，从**政治科学**及**管理科学**的理论上讲，这是一个**选民意愿表达及表达管理**的课题。那么如何让选民正确表达自己的意愿呢？如何对选民意愿的表达方式进行管理呢？ 下面我就示威游行这种意愿表达方式陈述本人的观点：

示威游行的民主权利可谓是历史悠久，其特点是**声势浩大，参与面广，影响力大**。然而，就意愿表达来讲，并不是每一个参与者都知道其本人的意愿表达和集体的意愿表达。因此，正确的做法是：每一次示威游行都应当有**意愿表达书（请愿书）**，应当有**送达对象**（**政府，立法机关**或其他相关机构），意愿表达书应适当公开。送达对象应当对意愿表达书在一定时间内给与恰当的回复。同时，每一次示威游行应当在公众媒体中公开其组织者及时间安排。这样就可以有一个**相互约束的机制**，从而使选民可以更理性的享有自己的民主权利。

另外一方面，示威游行不可以没有节制的持续进行， 否则就是对民主权利的滥用，对其他选民民主权利的伤害。因此在时间上应当对示威游行加以限制，举例讲，**一个星期，两个**

星期，等等。这样就可以尽最大可能的减少示威游行可能带来的负面影响。

当然，如果能够有一种**国际参与的机制**，可以对于强权政治或问题政府施加压力，那将是更好的选择，但却有干涉内政的嫌疑。

总之，对于示威游行这种意愿表达方式要完善，管理的方式也要完善。从而减少由示威游行而带来的社会动荡及国际负担。但愿我的主张能够得到**阿拉伯国家，欧洲国家**及其他饱受示威游行之困的国家的广泛的支持和拥护。

Sunday, March 23, 2014

<<Bird View>>

Win Your Heart

[赢得你的心]

I will not capture your body with my hands, but I will capture your heart with my heart no matter you are my friend or enemy.

我不会用我的手俘获你的身体，但我会用我的真心俘获你的真心，不管你是我的朋友还是敌人。

Saturday, March 15, 2014

<<Bird View>>

Politics - Strategy - On Political Opportunism and Political Utilitarianism

[政治 - 策略 - 论政治投机和政治功利主义]

Air Roller Coaster by Beizhan Liu

Political opportunism refers to short-term behavior on political strategy, which is to take some kind actions for the immediate benefit opportunity in spite of long-term interests.

Political utilitarianism refers to using the government's rights to influence and pursue common interests of all members of society on political morality, which is referred to the greatest happiness and joys of individual social member on moral utilitarianism. (See details in Jianxiao

Yang's Ph.D thesis <<On Political utilitarianism>> in Jilin University's the eighth period of 2009 of <<Ph.D Thesis>>)

In modern society management, the political systems in most countries belong to political utilitarianism. But because many countries are multiparty country, **approaches** advocated by various political groups are different, although the **goals** are the same. In political approaches advocated by some people, there may be a kind behavior of political opportunism.

Since most countries are political utilitarianism country, then, the behavior against the political utilitarianism is obviously not an advocate of society's main body, and will not be agreed by the most people of a society.

In terms of political opportunism, there are two **possible outcomes**. One is that speculators promptly adjust their political strategy after achieving success to restore the damage to their long-term interests. One is that speculators insist on their strategy without making any adjustments.

More realistic to speak, country in between country groups or major powers, if **taking the political opportunism strategy under the guidance of political utilitarian**, it would be a better choice.

政治投机是指在政治策略上的短期行为，即不顾及长远利益为眼前一时的利益机会而采取某些行动。

<<Bird View>>

政治功利主义是指政治道德上主张以政府的权利来影响和追求全体社会成员的普遍利益，也就是道德功利主义上所指的社会成员个体的最大的幸福和快乐。（详见吉林大学［博士论文]2009 年第 08 期 杨健潇博士论文<<论政治功利主义>>）

在现代社会管理中，多数国家的政治体制均属于政治功利主义。但由于许多国家都是多党制的国家，不同政治集团所主张的**途径**是不同的，尽管其**目标**是一致的。在某些人所主张的政治途径之中，就有可能是属于政治投机行为。

既然大多数国家是政治功利主义的国家，那么，违背政治功利主义的行为显然不是一个社会主体所倡导的，不是一个社会多数人所赞同的。

就政治投机而言，一般可能会有**两种结果**。一种是投机人在成功之后及时调整政治策略，从而挽回对其长期利益的伤害。一种是投机人坚持其策略，而不做任何调整。

更现实的讲，处于国家集团或大国之间的国家，如果采取在**政治功利主义指导下的政治投机**，那将是较好的选择。

Saturday, March 1, 2014

On "Principle of Universal Jurisdiction"

[论"普遍管辖原则"]

Recently I learned an anecdote from the news: the court in one country (X country) issued an order to want and arrest a number of former national leaders in a big country (Z country), and its basis was based on the remarks of one of its citizen who lived in the country (X country) for many years and the so-called **principle of universal jurisdiction**. Not to mention the **legal eligibility** of the prosecutor, just said the so-called principle of universal jurisdiction, its legitimacy in international management and international legal system is worth to question.

Since the country appeared in human history, **international management** is based on country as a unit, which is the so-called **national sovereignty**. Later, with the advent and expansion of the international exchanges and international disputes, regional and global international organization emerged gradually. **International management** was gradually expanded to international organizations from country management based on mutual authorization (Treaty), such as the **United Nations**.

National sovereignty includes the territorial sovereignty, the airspace sovereignty and the territorial sea sovereignty of a country, the country's legislative, judicial and executive powers. The legal foundation of a country's legislative and judicial power within its national sovereignty is usually presented as a country's **constitution law** or **basic law**. **Diplomatic relation** between countries is often firstly based on mutual recognition of national sovereignty.

The principle of universal jurisdiction extends the jurisdiction right out of the range as defined in the national sovereignty. While the constitution law or basic law of any country has the first priority right for interpretation and decision. No other laws can be above the Constitution Law or Basic Law. Then the so-called principle of universal jurisdiction is contrary to its own constitution law, **is illegal**.

The principle of universal jurisdiction across the defined sovereignty, conducts legal rulings on other country's affairs, is a kind **violation of judicial power** of other country. For the countries with diplomatic relation by mutual recognition of each others' national sovereignty, this kind violation of justice is a **behavior of breach of contract**, a kind of **behavior of denying diplomatic**

relation.

The principle of universal jurisdiction breaks the legal system of national management and international management since ancient times, the result can only bring chaos to the international management, bring damages to the country's **international reputation** and bring harms the country's **diplomatic relation**, and further hurts its national interests.

The across sovereignty justice rights must be based on mutual authorization (**treaty**) basis, such as the **International Court of Justice.**

Therefore, it is expected that X country can improve its own legal system, respects the national management and international management standards, respects the national sovereignty of the country with which it has diplomatic relation, makes due contributions for the improvement of rational order of international management.

最近从新闻中了解到这样一件奇闻：某一个国家（X 国）的法院竟然裁决要通缉并逮捕某一个大国（Z 国）的多位前国家领导人，而其依据是基于一个居住于其本国（X 国）多年的本国公民的陈词以及所谓的**普遍管辖原则**。　且不说起诉人的**法律资格**问题，单说所谓的普遍管辖原则，其在国际管理及国际法律体系中的合法性就值得置疑。

自从人类历史上国家出现以来，**国际管理**就是以国家为单元来进行管理的，这也就是所谓的**国家主权**。后来随着国际交往的扩大以及国际争端的出现，才逐步出现地区或全球性质的国际组织。**国际管理**才逐步由国家管理扩大到基于相互授权（条约）的国际组织管理，例如**联合国**。

国家主权包括对于本国领土，领空及领海的主权，对于本国的立法权，司法权和行政管理权。国家主权中立法权和司法权的法律基础通常是一个国家的**宪法**或**基本法**。国家与国家的**外交关系**通常是首先建立在相互承认国家主权的基础之上的。

普遍管辖原则将本国的司法权延伸扩张到了其本国主权所限定的范围之外，而任何一个国家的宪法或基本法都是拥有第一优先的解释权或决定权的。任何其他的法律都是不可以凌驾于宪法或基本法之上的。因此所谓的普遍管辖原则是违背其本国宪法的，**是违法的**。

普遍管辖原则跨越主权的限定，对其他国家的事物进行法律裁决是对于其他国家**司法权的一种侵犯**。对于相互承认各自国家主权并拥有外交关系的国家来言，这种司法的侵犯是一种**违约的行为**, 是一种**否认外交关系的行为**。

普遍管辖原则打破了自古以来的国家管理以及国际管理的法律体系，其结果只能是为国际管理带来混乱，给其本国的**国际信誉**及**外交关系**带来伤害，并进一步伤及其国家的利益。

跨越主权的司法权利一定是建立在相互授权（**条约**）的基础之上的，例如**国际法院**。

因此，望 X 国完善本国的法律体系，尊重国家管理及国际管理的准则， 尊重邦交国的国家主权，为完善国际管理的合理秩序做出应有的贡献。

Sunday, February 16, 2014

Rich & Poor

[富贵与贫穷]

In this world, no matter in which country, there are differences between the rich and the poor; there are rich people and poor people. Even the best social system can not eliminate the gap between the rich and the poor. But anyway, it is necessary for all of us to create the necessary conditions to share the wealth for the general public in the process of social wealth creation and circulation. **I hope the poor to be rich, but I do not want the rich to be poor.**

在这个世界上，无论是哪一个国家，都存在富贵和贫穷的差别；都有穷人和富人。 即使是最好的社会体制，也无法消除贫富的差距。但无论如何，我们都有必要在社会财富的创造和流通的过程中，尽可能的为普通大众分享财富创造必要的条件。我希望穷人变得富裕起来，但我并不希望富人变得穷困起来。

Sunday, February 9, 2014

Face Philosophy - The Lack of Self

[脸谱哲学 - 自我的缺失]

In social life, especially in political life, we will find that there are many characters have more or less similarities in appearance. Such similarities are historic or regional. This phenomenon occurs not only in China, but also in the world.   So   why   is   this?

Of course, first of all, people's appearances are born, unless you do cosmetic surgery. The human genes for the appearance may be limited, so the possibility of the similar appearance   is   very   high.

Secondly, perhaps the more important reason is that countries or organizations **judge by appearance when hiring** in order to express their political leaning and in order to maintain their influence or commercial interest.

However, judging by appearance when hiring, is clearly undesirable. On hiring, **we shall use what talents are good at and avoid what they are not good at**, we shall use **talents with both capability and integrity**, we shall use talents with probity and dedication to the public, we shall use **outspoken talents with impartiality**, we shall **use talents according to their capacity**, this is **the fundamental rule for hiring talents.**

Over emphasizing on the similarity of appearance, attention to so called **face philosophy**, is an indication of lack of self, is an indication of lack of confidence. It is the **lack of self.**

在社会生活中，尤其是在政治生活中，我们会发现有许多人物在相貌上具有或多或少的相似性。这种相似或者是历史性的，或者是地区性的。这种现象不仅出现在中国，更出现在世界。那么为什么会是这样的呢？

当然，首先，人的相貌是天生的，除非你去做整容手术。人类相貌的基因可能是有限的，因此出现相似性相貌的可能性是很高的。

其次，这也许是更重要的原因，那就是国家或机构为了表达自己的政治倾向以维护自己的影响力或商业利益，**在用人上，以貌取人。**

然而，在用人上，以貌取人，显然是不可取的。在用人上，要用人所长，**避人所短**，要用**德才兼备**之人，要用**廉洁奉公**之人，要用**直言秉公**之人，要量才适用，这才是**用人之道的根本**。

过分强调相貌的相似性，讲究所谓的**脸谱哲学**，是一种缺乏自我的表现，是一种缺乏自信的表现，是**自我的缺失**。

Sunday, January 19, 2014

The Life Long History of the Honesty and Social Responsibility of Chinese People (2)

[中国人的诚信和社会责任感的源远历史(2)]

Plum Blossoms by John Morgan (https://flic.kr/p/jzEcLc)

In the previous article I mainly talked about the integrity of Chinese people, I would like to talk about Chinese people's sense of social responsibility in this article. Some people may think that Chinese people lack social responsibility, either because of a bias, or because of little knowledge on China and Chinese people.

First, from the historical perspective, we can experience the sense of Chinese people's social responsibility from the two **well-known** stories. As you may know the story of **Mulan**, a woman who take the risk of sin and behead to join the army to protect her country, what is the motivation? It was her strong sense of social responsibility. And more, **Yuefei**'s mother engraved letters on his back, **Loyalty to and Serve Your Country**, what is the motivation? But also is a strong sense of social responsibility.

Second, from the domestic point of view, Chinese people's sense of social responsibility can be said is reflected in all aspects, not only in the executives, but also in ordinary people; reflected not only in the military, but also in the people.

China is a developing country, is not a developed country yet. China has vast territory with large population. China is also a country prone to natural disasters, especially floods in the central and south and drought in the north. When you opened a Chinese newspaper and look at the news pictures while every major natural disaster happened, you will feel the strong sense of social responsibility of Chinese people. Chinese has an old saying called: "**A difficult one, Help comes from all**". It means that **human being is social human being; social responsibility is the social instinct of human being**. In the past, the most shocking photo when the Yangtze River flood happened was the affecting scene that then President Jiang Zemin directed the flood fighting on site. When the shocked the world Wenchuan earthquake occurred, then President Hu Jintao and Premier Wen Jiabao also went to the scene to direct and to express sympathy. During every major danger, what we saw most was the presence of the military, they always **suffered first, sacrificed first**. As for ordinary people, they even gave more supports and assistances within their capacities. For example speaking, overseas Chinese gave a lot of donations when each major natural disaster happened in China.

My hometown has often suffered flood dangers, once the flood came, really **all were soldiers**. I was also on the levee to inspect while I was in very young age. I remember one time that the flood was too hard, we had to sacrifice the countryside to protect the city. So the river levee on the countryside was blown up. Of course, all the people in the village had been withdrawn. So the Chinese people's sense of social responsibility is also reflected in the **spirit of sacrifice**.

Again from an international perspective, Chinese people's sense of social responsibility is reflected in the concern and support to the neighboring countries and least developed countries. I remember that China have sent a lot of medical teams to Africa to support African friends. Of course I don't know a lot about this. I will not say more.

The same word, any society is not perfect, judgment should be based on the universality and mainstream of a country and a society. In short, Chinese people's integrity virtue and the sense of social responsibility have life long history.

在前面的文章中主要谈到了中国人的诚信，在这篇文章中我再来谈一谈中国人的社会责任感。某些人认为中国人缺乏社会责任感，要么是一种偏见，要么是由于对中国和中国人了解不多。

首先从历史的角度来看，我们可以从两个**众人皆知**的故事来体会中国人社会责任感。大家也许都知道**花木兰**的故事，一个女性冒杀头之罪从军，保护国家，什么动机？ 就是其社会责任感的强烈意识。还有**岳母刺字，精忠报国**，什么动机？也是其社会责任感的强烈意识。

其次从国内的角度来看，中国人的社会责任感可以说体现在方方面面，不仅体现在管理者，更体现在普通百姓；不仅体现在军，更体现在民。

中国是一个发展中国家，还并不是一个发达国家。中国幅员辽阔，人口众多。中国也是自然灾害频发的国家，尤其是中南部的洪水和北方的干旱。翻开中国的报纸，看一看每次重大自然灾害发生时的新闻图片，你就会强烈地感受到中国人的社会责任意识。中国有句古话叫做："**一方有难，八方支援**"，说的就是**人是一个社会的人，社会责任是人之社会本能**。想当年，长江洪水发生时最震撼的一张照片就是当时的国家主席江泽民亲自指挥抗洪的感人镜头。震惊世界的汶川大地震发生时，当时的国家主席胡锦涛和总理温家宝也都亲赴现场指挥和慰问。每次重大险情，看到最多的身影就是军人，他们总是**吃苦在先，牺牲在先**。至于普通百姓，则更是给与力所能及的支持和帮助，举个例子讲，每次国内重大自然灾害，海外华人都给与了不少的捐赠。

我的家乡也曾经常遭遇洪水的险情，一旦洪水来临，可真是**全民皆兵**，那时年龄很小的我也在大堤上巡视。记得有一次洪水太大，只好牺牲农村，保护城市，将河对面的大堤给炸了，当然村里的人全都给撤了。所以中国人的社会责任感还体现在**牺牲精神**上。

再次从国际的角度来看，中国人的社会责任感体现在对周边国家及不发达国家的关心及支援。 我记得中国曾经向非洲派

出了很多医疗队以支持非洲的朋友。当然这方面，我了解的
情况不多。我就不多说了。

还是那句话：任何一个社会都不是尽善尽美的，要依据一个
国家，一个社会的普遍性和主流来做判断。总之，中国人的
社会责任感和诚信美德是有源远历史的。

Saturday, January 4, 2014

Thinking about President LBJ

[论 LBJ 总统]

Lyndon Baines Johnson President by Cliff
(https://www.flickr.com/photos/nostri-imago/2872024078)

Recently, when I studied the modern history of United States, I suddenly and surprisingly found an American president who I never know before: Lyndon B. Johnson. Among the U.S. presidents, John F. Kennedy was **well known, known to everybody** in China. But Lyndon Johnson, not many people know about him. I was surprised not only because that I did not know him before, but also because of his so great achievements and contributions to the modern American society during his tenure. Perhaps it can be said that modern American society began to take shape in his era.

The thinking of "**Great Society**" proposed by President Lyndon Johnson made a very realistic response to the needs of American society at that time. Modern government public service sector perhaps started to build up under this thinking, for example saying, the government-funded education and employment programs. Of course, the thinking of "Great Society" contained many aspects: **health care, urban renewal and beautification, the development of underdeveloped areas, large-scale anti-poverty war, the prevention and control of crime**, as well as **the vote right reform**.

President Lyndon Johnson pioneered **the equal suffrage** in modern America. He was also a pioneer in **racial equality**. The <<**Civil Rights Act**>> passed in 1964 made it illegal racial discrimination and segregation. The <<**Voting Rights Act**>> passed in 1965 made people of different skin colors to gain equal voting rights, especially the U.S. blacks.

The <<**Immigration Law**>> signed by President Lyndon Johnson in 1965 made the U.S. immigration policy from facing Europe to facing the world. This laid a foundation for the internationalization of U.S.

President Lyndon Johnson's contribution to **education** in

United States was huge. He believes that education is the panacea for anti-poverty and personal growth, is an essential element of **the American Dream**. The **<<Elementary and Secondary Education Act>>** and **<<Higher Education Act>>** in 1965 issued under his leadership should be the cornerstones for the basic education and higher education of modern American Society.

President Lyndon Johnson's contribution to the American humanities, arts and the media was that he established **the National Endowment for the Humanities** and **the National Endowment for the Arts** as well as the **<<Public Broadcasting Act>>** signed in 1967 by him.

In respect of anti-poverty, in 1964, the Congress passed the **<<Tax Act>>** and the **<<Economic Opportunity Act>>** upon his request. In his tenure, the percentage of Americans living below the poverty line fell from 23% to 12%.

In **healthcare**, the Medicare program was established on July   30,   965.

On the other hand, the **Internet** was also successfully developed by the ARPANET program in his era.

I think perhaps he was the American president who signed most   bills   in   modern   America   history.

Of course, in his tenure, there had been very serious urban violence, as well as upgraded Vietnam War, which added a lot of dark colors to his glorious image. It was not known for the reasons behind these events.

I hope that those who, like me, do not know much about President Lyndon Johnson thus to be able to learn more about him, so as to have more objective and comprehensive understanding on American society.

最近，我在了解美国近代历史的时候，忽然吃惊地发现一个我过去从不知道的美国总统，即林登·约翰逊。在美国总统里边，约翰·肯尼迪在中国几乎**无人不知，无人不晓**。但对林登·约翰逊了解的人却不多。我吃惊的不仅在于我过去了解他，更在于他在任内的成就及对美国现代社会的贡献如此之大。也许可以说美国现代社会就是在他那个时代开始成型的。

林登·约翰逊总统提出的**"伟大社会"**的思想非常切合实际的反映了当时美国社会的需求。现代的政府公共服务部门也许就是在这一思想的主导下开始建立起来的，举例讲，政府资助的教育及就业项目。当然，"伟大社会"的思想包含很多方面，**医疗保健，城市重建及美化，对不发达地区的开发，大规模的反贫**，对于犯罪的预防及控制，还有**选举权的改革**。

林登·约翰逊总统开创了美国现代**平等选举**的先河。是**种族平等**的先驱。1964 年通过的《**民权法案**》使得种族歧视和种族隔离成为非法。1965 年通过的《**投票权法案**》使得不同肤色的国民都获得了同等的投票权，尤其是美国的黑人。

林登·约翰逊总统 1965 年签署的《**移民法**》使得美国的移民政策由面向欧洲转向面向世界。从而为美国的国际化打下了基础。

林登·约翰逊总统对美国**教育**的贡献也是巨大的。他认为教育是反贫和个人成长的灵丹妙药，是美国梦的基本要素。1965年在他主导下所通过的《小学和中学教育法》及《高等教育法》应该是美国现代社会基础教育及高等教育的奠基石。

林登·约翰逊总统对与美国人文，艺术和媒体的贡献在于他建立了**美国国家人文基金会**和**美国国家艺术基金会**以及通过了《公共广播法》。

在反贫方面，1964 年在他的主导下国会通过了《税收法案》和《经济机会法》 。在他的任内，美国人生活在贫困线以下的比例从 23% 下降到了 12%。

在**医疗保健**方面，1965 年 7 月 30 日建立了医疗保健项目。

另外一个方面，**互联网**也是在他这个时期由 ARPANET 项目开发成功的。

我觉得他也许是美国近代**签署法案最多**的美国总统。

当然，在他的任内也出现了很严重的城市暴力事件，还有升级的越战，这为他的光辉形象增添了不少灰暗的色彩。至于这些事件背后的原因就不可而知了。

我希望那些像我一样不了解林登·约翰逊总统的人能够由此对他有更多的了解，从而对美国社会有更客观，更全面的认识。

Saturday, December 21, 2013

The Life Long History of the Honesty and Social Responsibility of Chinese People (1)

[中国人的诚信和社会责任感的源远历史(1)]

Plum Blossoms By John Morgan (https://flic.kr/p/jzEcLc)

Due to individual event or individual misconduct of some Chinese people, Chinese people's integrity and social responsibility were doubted to some degree in the eyes of some people, and thus suspect the traditional Chinese virtues. Therefore, it is necessary to recall the history of the virtues of Chinese people's integrity and social responsibility, and introduce some interesting stories, so that we can have a better understanding on Chinese people, so as to increase trust and friendship. Let me first talk about the Chinese people's integrity.

First, from many Chinese idioms and old sayings, you can

appreciate the history of Chinese people's integrity, for
example:

"Sincerity, heaven's truth; sincere thinking, people's truth."
---- **Mencius** (BC 372 - BC 289);

"No trust, no standing for a people." ---- **Confucius** (552 BC
October 9 - 479 BC March 9);

"Unbelievable words will result nothing in action." ---- **Mo
Tzu** (479 BC - 381 BC);

"Stand by what you say, Result by what you do." ---- **Zi Lu**
(542 BC - 480 BC);

"Honesty, the foundation for the five virtues, the source for
all trades." ---- **Zhou dunyi** (1017-1073);

"You cannot lead your people without believe, you cannot
guard your country without your people." ----
<<General View for Country Management>> (1019-1086);

"Once a word is out, four horses cannot catch it back." ----
Chinese Proverb;

"A word is like nine tripods." ---- **Feng guifen** (1809~1874);

See http://www.fyeedu.net/info/157281-1.htm

Second, China has a lot of historical stories about the

integrity. Due to the limited space, here I only introduce one:

The founding father of **Han Dynasty**, **Han Xin** (In 231 BC - 196 BC), was very poor in his childhood, he often lived without food and clothing. He followed his older brother and his sister-in-law, lived on eating leftovers. The little Han Xin worked during the day to help his brother, and studied hard in the evening, harsh sister-in-law hated his reading because it took a lot of kerosene and was useless. Then Han Xin had to live on the streets **with no adequate clothing** and **no enough food.** An old lady who was a servant for others was very sympathetic to him and supported his reading. She gave him eating everyday. Han Xin was very grateful to this old lady, he said:" I must repay you when I grow up." The old lady smiled and said: "When you grow up I was buried." Later Han Xin turned out to be a famous general, and was crowned as the king of Chu by Liu Bang (Emperor of Han Dynasty), he still missed the old lady who had ever helped him. Then he found the old lady and received her to his own palace. He treated her as his mother.

See http://u.sanwen.net/subject/1003025.html

The integrity is a vital ethical standard for every country, every nation and every individual. It is the moral foundation for the prosperity of a country, the strength of a nation and the development of a person. Chinese people attach a great importance on integrity virtue education from ancient to today. Whether in family education, social education, or in school education, all emphasize on the cultivation of moral integrity. Of course, no one is perfect, any society is not perfect; judgment should be based on the universality and mainstream of a country and a society. In short, Chinese people's integrity virtue has life long history.

由于个别的事件或个别中国人的不轨行为，使得中国人的诚信和社会责任感在某些人的眼里受到一定的质疑，并由此怀疑中国人的传统美德。因此，很有必要回顾一下中国人诚信美德和社会责任感的历史，并介绍一些趣闻故事，让大家对中国人有更深入的了解，以增加信任，增进友谊。我首先来谈谈中国人的诚信。

首先，从中国的很多成语及古语中，就可以体会到中国人诚信的源远历史，例如：

"诚者，天之道也；思诚者，人之道也 。" ---- **孟子** （公元前 372 年－公元前 289 年）；
"民无信不立" ---- **孔子**（公元前 552 年 10 月 9 日－公元前 479 年 3 月 9 日）；
"言不信者，行不果" ---- **墨子**（公元前 479 年－公元前 381 年）；
"言必信，行必果。" ---- **子路** （公元前 542 年－公元前 480 年）；
"诚，五常之本，百行之源也。" ---- **周敦颐**（1017-1073）；
"非信无以使民，非民无以守国。" ---- 《**资治通鉴**》）（1019-1086）；
"一言既出，驷马难追。" ---- **中国谚语**；
"一言九鼎" ---- **冯桂芬**(1809～1874)；

详见 http://www.fyeedu.net/info/157281-1.htm

其次，中国还有很多有关诚信的历史故事，限于篇幅，这里只给大家介绍一个：

汉朝的开国功臣**韩信**(约公元前 231 年－公元前 196 年)，幼时家里很贫穷，常常衣食无着，他跟着哥哥嫂嫂住在一起，靠吃剩饭剩菜过日子。小韩信白天帮哥哥干活，晚上刻苦读书，刻薄的嫂嫂非常讨厌他读书，认为读书耗费了灯油，又没有用处。于是韩信只好流落街头，过着**衣不蔽体，食不裹腹**的生活。有一位为别人当佣人的老婆婆很同情他，支持他读书，还每天给他饭吃。面对老婆婆的一片诚心，韩信很感激，他对老人说：“我长大了一定要报答你。”，老婆婆笑着说：“等你长大后我就入土了。”， 后来韩信成为著名的将领，被刘邦(汉朝的皇帝)封为楚王，他仍然惦记着这位曾经给他帮助的老人。他于是找到这位老人，将老人接到自己的宫殿里，像对待自己的母亲一样对待她。

详见 http://u.sanwen.net/subject/1003025.html

诚信对于每一个国家，每一个民族，每一个人都是至关重要的道德标准。是国家兴盛，民族富强， 个人发展的道德基础。中国人自古至今都非常重视诚信道德的教育。无论在家庭教育，社会教育，还是在校园教育，都无不强调诚信道德的培养。当然，人无完人， 任何一个社会都不是尽善尽美的；要依据一个国家，一个社会的普遍性和主流来做判断。总之，中国人的诚信美德是有源远历史的。

Saturday, December 14, 2013

The Long Live History of the Legal Spirit Of Great China

[中国法制精神的源远历史]

Police Before Tian An Men by ©Bilwander
(https://www.flic.kr/p/7k1T1C)

Westerners may not know much about the history of China's legal system, most people think that China has always been a people powered country which is represented by the emperor system. In fact, the spirit of China's legal system also has a long history, can be said as a long live history. In the Warring States Period (lower half of the 5th century BC), **<<LAW SCRIPTURE>>**, which was enacted by the famous reformer **Kui Li**, was the first comparatively systematic feudalism written law in the history of China. There are six chapters in **<<LAW**

SCRIPTURE>>: <<Pirates Law>>, <<Thieves Law>>, <<Prison Law>>, <<Catch Law>>, <<Miscellaneous Law>>, <<Conviction and Sentencing Law>>. After **Kui Li, Yang Shang** carried <<LAW SCRIPTURE>> and went into state of Qin and started the political reform movement, which had laid a stable internal management foundation for Qin's unification of China. In Han Dynasty, **He Xiao** added another three chapters on the basis of <<LAW SCRIPTURE>>, which were <<Households>>, <<Business>>, <<Livestock>>, and made it into the Han Empire's <<IX Law>>. The <<Tang Law>> was written on the basis of <<IX Law>> and improved it.

The earliest written law in the Western, **<<Law of the Twelve Tables>>**, which was the origin and foundation of Roman Law Family, was also enacted in the 5th century BC. It was in the same era that <<LAW SCRIPTURE>> was enacted.

(See http://blog.ifeng.com/article/20873996.html)

The first constitution law in China's history was the <<Constitutional Outline>> in later year of Qing Dynasty, which was promulgated in August 1908. In the period of KMT, the national government formulated the <<Constitution of the Republic of China>>, probably promulgated in October 8, 1928. New China's first Constitution Law, **<<Constitution of the People's Republic of China>>** was promulgated on September 20, 1954.

<<Bird View>>

(See http://zh.wikipedia.org/wiki/ China Constitution)

The first law promulgated by New China was **<<Marriage Law>>**, which was promulgated on May 1, 1950. China has nearly **300** laws which are enacted by NPC and its Standing Committee and administrative regulations, nearly more than **800** regulations which are enacted by the State Council, as well as more than **28,000** pieces of regulations, more than **7,000** local regulations, autonomous regulations or specific regulations.

(See http://iask.sina.com.cn/b/2251802.html)

Of course, in China's history, there had been many war eras or special periods, in which the authority of the law was replaced by the personal authority of warlords or local separatist forces, the law was no longer respected, the legal system was replaced by the personal power. Such periods or eras also existed in the history of the Western.

I am here to briefly explain the origin of China's Law Family, I hope that this can provide a basic understanding of China's legal system, which may be a kind help to our work and prevent joke making.

西方人对于中国的法制历史可能了解不多，多数人认为中国历来就是一个以皇帝为代表的人制国家。其实不然，中国的法制精神也有很悠久的历史，可谓源远流长。

在战国时期（公元前 5 世纪下半叶）由著名的改革家**李悝**所制定的**《法经》**是中国历史上第一部比较系统的封建成文法

典。《法经》共有六篇：《盗法》，《贼法》，《囚法》，《捕法》，《杂法》，《具法》。

在**李悝**之后，**商鞅**携《**法经**》入秦并实行变法运动，为秦国统一中国奠定了内部管理的稳定基础。在汉朝，**萧何**在《**法经**》六篇的基础上增加户、兴、厩三篇，使其转化为大汉帝国的《**九章律**》。而《**唐律**》又是在汉朝《**九章律**》的基础上完善撰写的。

西方最早的法典，也就是罗马法系的起源和基础的法典《**十二铜表法**》也产生于公元前 5 世纪。是和《**法经**》产生于同样的年代。

（详见 http://blog.ifeng.com/article/20873996.html）

中国历史上第一部宪法是清朝末年的《**钦定宪法大纲**》，它诞生于 1908 年 8 月。在国民党时期，国民政府制定了《**中华民国宪法**》，大概诞生于 1928 年 10 月 8 日。新中国的第一部宪法《**中华人民共和国宪法**》诞生于 1954 年 9 月 20 日。

（详见 http://zh.wikipedia.org/wiki/中华宪法）

新中国颁布的第一部法律是《**婚姻法**》。颁行于 1950 年 5 月 1 日。中国现有近 **300** 个全国人大及其常委会制定的法律，近 800 多个国务院的行政法规，还有 **28000** 多件规章，**7000** 多个地方性法规、自治条例和单行条例。

（详见 http://iask.sina.com.cn/b/2251802.html）

当然，在中国的历史上曾经出现过很多战乱的年代或特殊的时期，在那些年代或时期，法律的权威被军阀或地方割据势

力的个人权威所替代，法律不再受到尊重，法制为人制所取
代。这样的年代或时期在西方也是存在的。

我在这里简单介绍一下中华法系的渊源，希望大家冀此对中
华法系有所了解，对大家的工作能有一些帮助，不要闹出笑
话来。

Saturday, November 30, 2013

Energy and New Energy

[能源与新能源]

Street Car by Beizhan Liu

In the field of international energy development and application, the controversy of new energy or renewable energy and traditional energy or non-renewable energy is very intense. Exactly at what kind pace shall we promote and apply new energy? With what kind pace and measure shall we deal with the challenge from new energy for the traditional energy? It is an unavoidable topic for every leader of the energy industry and energy state.

The interest of traditional energy industry has to be protected; the application of new energy should also be gradually expanded. Avoiding either aspect is all wrong. Since new energy has incomparable advantages over traditional energy, new energy is bound to gradually become the protagonist of the future energy application. This is a trend of social development, and cannot be transferred upon individual's will. Of course, this is a very long process.

The pioneer officer country in new energy application process will definitely dominate the future energy technology. Therefore, traditional energy countries have to pay more attention to the development and application of new energy. Traditional energy country's energy industry shall plan to face the challenge and gradually change the role in a longer period, in order to avoid possible losses. This is called being **prepared to avoid risk**.

在国际能源开发和应用的领域中，新能源或者说可再生能源与传统能源或者说不可再生能源的争议很激烈。我们究竟应当以什么样的步伐来推广和应用新能源， 我们又应当以什么样的步伐和措施来应对新能源对传统能源的挑战呢？这是每一个能源工业以及能源国家领导人所不可回避的课题。

传统能源工业的利益要得到保护，新能源的应用也要逐步展开。回避任何一个方面都是错误的。由于新能源具有传统能源所不可比拟的优势，新能源必然会逐步成为未来能源应用的主角。这是一个社会发展的趋势，是不以个人的意志为转移的。当然这是一个很长的过程。

在新能源应用的过程中担当先锋官的国家一定会主导未来的能源技术。因此，传统能源国家更要关注新能源的开发和应用。传统能源国家的能源工业应该在一个较长阶段内有计划地面对挑战，逐步转变角色， 以避免可能带来的损失。这就叫做**有备无患**。

Thursday, November 14, 2013

Don't Cry! Oil Sands! - North America Energy Safety

[不要哭泣！油沙！－北美能源安全]

Pair of Tulip by Beizhan Liu

Recent years, I always heard the reports on oil sands and pipeline across United States from the media. For the oil and energy industry, I myself know very little, I have not much interest. As an outsider, I'm wondering why Canada is going to build so long oil pipeline in United States, it costs a lot of money, it can create a lot of employment opportunities for Americans. However, Americans do not appreciate this for Canada; United States does not want to build such a pipeline. Do not say that such a pipeline should be built or not, obviously North America's energy planning and management lack co-ordination aspect.

Canada and United States, as North America's largest two neighboring countries, have to keep consistent pace in many areas, after all they are the nearest. Canada and United States have co-management model in other areas. There should have some kind coordinated planning in the energy sector. There should be an **energy security coordination committee** to operate. If Alaska oil is going to be transported to United States, it may be impossible not to go through Canada. The large pipeline should be established by large multi-party beneficiaries. Of course, this depends on the feasibility of commercial operation. In short, overall planning and coordination management are necessary.

For oil sand mine, I advocate the development in case the environment is adequately protected, but I'm not in favor of aggressive exploitation. This is one aspect of my theory of limited economic growth.

Don't Cry! Oil Sands!

这些年来，总是从媒体中听到油沙矿以及横贯美国的输油管的报道。对于石油能源行业，我本人了解很少，兴趣也不大。作为一个局外人，我很纳闷的是为什么加拿大要修那么长的石油管线到美国，要花很多的钱，可以为美国人创造很多的就业机会。然而，美国人并不领情；并不希望加拿大在美国建这样的管线。却不说这样的管线该不该建，单说北美的能源计划与管理，显然缺乏统筹的一面。

加拿大和美国作为北美最大的两个相邻的国家，在很多方面不能不协调步伐，毕竟距离最近吗。加拿大和美国在其他方面有合作管理的样板，在能源领域也应该统筹计划，应该有一个能源安全协调委员会来操作。因为美国的阿拉斯加要输石油往美国的话，不经过加拿大，也许是不可能的。大型的管线应该有多方受益人共同建立。当然，这要看商业运作的可行性了。总之，统筹计划和协调管理是很有必要的。

对于油沙矿，我主张在环境得到充分保护的情况下开发，但我不主张过度开发。这也是我有限经济增长理论的一个方面。

不要哭泣！油沙！

Wednesday, November 6, 2013

Joint Venture - The Solution for Cross Border Resource Disputation

[合营－跨界资源争议的解决方案]

Bird in a Tree by Beizhan Liu

In international disputes, we often see such situation: the boundary of two neighboring countries is clear, but the underground mineral resources discovered are across two or more countries, especially for some of the flowing resources, such as: oil. How to handle such disputes properly is an important weight to test the good-neighborhood   relationship.

To handle such disputes properly and maintain long-term good-neighborhood relationship, the best way is to establish joint venture and to explore the resource jointly. The benefits can be shared by all the circumstances according to the share of resources. This way can save development and investment costs for all parties. Such a solution should be relatively fair, is more commercially viable and workable.

在国际纷争中，我们经常会看到这样的情形：两个相邻的国家的边界是清楚的，但地下所发现的矿藏资源却是横跨两个或多个国家的，尤其是对于一些流动性的资源，例如：石油。对于这样的争议，如何正确处理，是考验邻邦睦邻友好关系的一个重要的砝码。

要正确处理这样的争议，保持长久的睦邻友好关系，最好的办法就是合资经营，共同开发。利益按资源所有情况而共同享有，同时也可以节省双方的开发投入成本。这样的解决办法应该是比较公正，在商业上也是比较可行的，可操作的。

Wednesday, October 30, 2013

The Analysis of the Creativity and Competitiveness between USA and Canada （1）

[美国和加拿大的创造力和竞争力分析(1)]

Right Wing of BOSS Table by Beizhan Liu

The different aspects of creativity and competitiveness of United States and Canada, two great powers in North America, are very interesting, and are well worth to analyze. In some respects, Canada's creativity is not worse than that of United States, there are a lot of things created here in Canada or first owned here, but United State was able to come from behind to win Canada in terms of competition. For examples, FLICKR was created in Canada, and later acquired by American's YAHOO. But then the Americans use the similar thinking behind FLICKR, and developed a lot of online services, such as: YOUTUBE, SLIDESHARE, PINTEREST, etc. They all achieved great success. Here is another example, Canada has POF, the Americans later developed TAGGED, in fact, they are similar things, but TAGGED achieved more success in the commercial market and product design. Such examples could be many.

There is also another very interesting phenomenon that some of America's major achievements made by people who actually are from Canada, for example: JAVA language creator JAMES GOSLING.

It would appear that Canadians are not worse than Americans in creativity, and even may lead it. However, Americans always prevail over the competition in the market. This phenomenon can not but reflects on. It is imperative for the relevant government departments to analyze seriously, find out the reasons, so that the creative businesses or individuals can also be more competitive on the market. This is also an issue related with the competitiveness of entire Canada. Canada shall take United State as an example to learn and follow in respect of competitiveness while keeping the leading position in respect of creativity, and take efforts to improve his own competitiveness.

美国和加拿大作为北美洲的两个大国在创造力和竞争力方面的不同是很有趣的，也是很值得分析的。在某些方面，加拿大的创造力并不比美国差，有很多东西 是加拿大这边创造的，先拥有的， 但美国却能够后来居上，在竞争力上取胜加拿大。 举例讲，加拿大先有 FLICKR，后来被美国的 YAHOO 收购了。但后来美国人采用类似于 FLICKR 的思路，开发了很多网上的服务，而且都很成功。再举例讲，加拿大有 POF, 美国人后来开发了 TAGGED， 其实都是类似的东西， 但 TAGGED 在商业市场上和产品设计上都要更胜一筹。 这样的例子可能还有很多。

另外还有一个很有趣的现象就是美国的某些作出重大成就的人其实是来自于加拿大，比如说：JAVA 语言的创造者 JAMES GOSLING。

这样看来，加拿大人在创造力上确实并不比美国人差，甚至还领先呢。但在市场竞争方面，占上风的却总是美国人。这种现象不能不令人反思。政府相关部门确实有必要认真分析，查找原因，让有创造力的企业或个人同样能够在市场上具有竞争力。这也是整个加拿大的竞争力所在。加拿大应该在保持创造力领先的同时， 在竞争力方面向美国学习，努力提高自我的竞争力。

Saturday, October 19, 2013

The Differentiation of Personal and Commercial

[个人与商业的区分]

Mini UAV by Beizhan Liu

In our daily life, we often see some terms with constraints emphasizing on personal and commercial distinction. I think, in some cases, it is acceptable to emphasize the difference between personal and commercial in terms of constraints, but in some circumstances it is unreasonable. This relates to the guiding principles for the legal practitioner to draft legal documents. I think an excellent legal practitioner shall consider the following guiding principles in drafting legal documents according to the following order of priority:

1). Terms of legal documents should first consider the social and public interests;

2). Terms of legal documents should first consider the interests of environment and resources;

3). Terms of legal documents should first consider the interests of customers;

4). Terms of legal documents should balance the interests of customers and businesses to the maximum;

5). Terms of legal documents should comply with the changed human society and public life due to the technology advancement to the maximum;

6). Then, the terms of the legal documents shall protect the business   interests   to   the   maximum;

7). Terms   of   legal   documents   must   be   binding.

Based on this, in what circumstances can we emphasize the difference between personal and commercial? Under what circumstances we can not emphasize the difference between   personal   and   commercial?

1). If it is difficult to distinguish personal and commercial for a commercial product or service in its application process or in some application environments, or the distinction will bring unnecessary waste of resources to the society and the public, there shall be no emphasizing on the difference between personal and commercial, for example: mobile phone, home internet and home phone.

2). If a term of legal document is hardly to be executed by every customer, then, that term is not a binding term, it is an invalid term. Invalid term has no legal significance.

Of course, each specific case shall be analyzed by the legal practitioners for the specific issue. I will not list them here one by one. In conclusion, I hope that **every legal document shall maximize the fairness and impartiality. This is the sacred duty of legal practitioner. We have the responsibility to make this world more rational, better and more beautiful.**

在我们日常生活中，我们时常看到一些约束条款中强调个人和商业的区别。我认为在某些情况下，在约束条款中强调个人和商业的区别是可以的， 但在某些情况下却是不合理的。这涉及到法律工作者起草法律文件时的主导原则。我认为一个优秀的法律工作者在起草法律文件时应按以下优先顺序考虑法律文件的主导原则：

1）。法律文件的条款应首先考虑社会及大众的利益；

2）。法律文件的条款应首先考虑环境及资源的利益；

3）。法律文件的条款应首先考虑消费者的利益；

4）。法律文件的条款应尽可能的平衡消费者和商家的利益；

5）。法律文件的条款应尽可能的符合因技术进步而改变了的人类社会和大众生活；

6）。在此之后，法律文件的条款才可以尽最大可能的保护商家的利益；

7）。法律文件的条款一定要有约束性；

基于此，在什么情况下可以强调个人与商业的区别呢？在什么情况下不可以强调个人与商业的区别呢？

1）。如果一个商业产品或服务在应用的过程中，或在某些应用的环境中很难对个人和商业加以区分， 或者如果加以区分则将给社会及大众带来不必要的资源的浪费。在此情况下，就不可以强调个人和商业的区别。举例讲：手机，家庭的互联网和家庭的电话。

2）。如果一个法律条款是几乎没有一个消费者能够执行的， 那么，该条款就是没有约束力的条款，也就是无效条款。无效条款是没有任何法律意义的。

当然，具体的还要每一个法律工作者具体问题具体分析。我就不在此一一列举了。 总之， 我希望**每一个法律文件都能够最大限度的体现公平和公正**。这也是**法律工作者的神圣职责**。我们有责任**让这个世界更合理，更完善， 更美好**。

Sunday, October 13, 2013

Culture - Wealth Hard To Create

[文化 - 难以创造的财富]

Table on the side of water by Beizhan Liu

Culture is not only the representation of the quintessence from our human being's wisdom, but also a kind wealth hard to create, especially under today's international background of the growing popularity of mass production and information technology. Saying this is because the expression of culture, especially the expression of the unique and distinctive culture is a rare way to accumulate wealth. For example, music and musicians can create great wealth, films and filmmakers can create great wealth, historical and cultural monuments can create great wealth either.

On the other hand, the creation of cultural product is quite difficult, because you need to be unique and to be accepted by most people. If the same, it is not your culture, it is far from creation. Of course, I am not encouraging excessive pursuit of cultural differences, because it is a very difficult thing. But if the pursuit of the same culture, it is clearly contrary to human creativity, and may lose the potential to create enormous wealth. We would like our human beings can be under the guidance of our wisdom, and create more cultures while accumulate more wealth.

文化既是人类智慧结晶的表现，更是一种难以创造的财富，尤其是在当今大规模生产及信息技术日益普及的国际背景下。 之所以这样说，是因为文化的展示，尤其是独有的，与众不同的文化的展示， 是一种不可多得的积累财富的途径。举例讲，音乐及音乐人可以创造巨大的财富，电影和电影人可以创造巨大的财富，历史的文化古迹也可以创造巨大的财富。

从另一方面讲，文化产品是很难创造的，因为你要与众不同， 并且能够为多数人所接受。 如果相同，那就不是你的文化， 那就谈不上创造。当然我也并不想鼓励过于追求文化的不同， 因为那是很难的事情。但是如果追求文化的相同，那显然是有悖于人类的创造性，并可能丧失可能创造的巨大财富。愿我们人类在智慧的引导下，创造更多的文化， 积累更多的财富。

Saturday, October 5, 2013

Review of the Spirit of America

[重温美国精神]

The Statue of Liberty

Recent years, multiple serious gun shooting cases happened in United States and caused numerous casualties among innocents. I am deeply saddened. As an ordinary people in the neighbor country of United States, I really cannot understand why such events can happen in the most developed United States, especially such events can happen in the key core departments? It's time to reflect truly.

United States is the most developed country in the world. The spirit of America is worshiped and admired by everyone. The stubborn pursuit of personal goals, create and progress, patriotism, pride and loyalty contained in the spirit of America are the driving force for all young people to mold themselves.

The recently happened cases obviously are out of tune with the spirit of America. Also, I think the spirit of America should include respect and pardon. Everyone may encounter one setback or another, or uneven, but in any case we have no reason to resort to violence, and to hurt innocents. We should respect others and respect for life. An advocate of violence in the society must be a deformed society; it must be a problem society.

Of course, to solve this problem, gun control is one very important aspect; propaganda and education are another two important aspects. Public opinion may not play up violence, and even advocate violence. Everyone shall look in the mirror, adjust his mentality and treat himself and others with peace. In short, I hope that similar vicious incidents do not occur again.

Here, I also would like to send the Americans three words sincerely: **Americans love Americans, Americans love America, Americans love the world**. And I hope every American can keep the three words in mind. Americans shall not only do their duty to build a peaceful and safe world, but also shall take their responsibility for the peace and security of United States. God bless America!

<<Bird View>>

最近这些年来，美国发生了多起严重的枪击案件，造成了众多无辜人员的伤亡。我对此深表痛心，作为美国邻邦的一位普通百姓，我很不能够理解为什么发达的美国会出现这样的情形，尤其是最近这种事件竟然会出现在关键的核心部门。实在是觉得应该反省一下了。

美国是世界上最发达的国家。美国精神更是大家所崇拜和仰慕的。美国精神所包含的顽强，追求个人理想，创造和进步，爱国，自豪及忠诚无不成为年轻人自我塑造的推动力量。

显然最近发生的这些事情和美国精神是格格不入的。而且，我认为美国精神还应当包含尊重和包容。每一个人都可能会遇到这样或那样的挫折或不平，但无论如何我们都没有理由诉诸暴力，伤及无辜。我们应当尊重他人，尊重生命。一个崇尚暴力的社会一定是一个畸形的社会；一定是一个有问题的社会。

当然，要解决这个问题，枪支管理是很重要的一个方面；宣传和教育是另外两个重要的方面。舆论导向不可以过于渲染暴力，甚至于鼓吹暴力。每一个人都应当自我反省，调整自己的心态，以平和的心情对待自己，对待他人。总之，我希望类似的恶性事件不要再次发生。

在此，我也衷心的送给美国人三句话：**美国人爱美国人，美国人爱美国，美国人爱世界**。并希望每一个美国人都能够牢记在心。美国人不仅要为建立一个和平安全的世界而尽自己的一份力量，更要为美国的和平安全而尽自己的职责。愿上帝保佑美国。

Sunday, September 22, 2013

Singing with Heart

[用心去唱]

Singing with your heart, then you can win the hearts of the audience, then you can win the true applauses from the audience.

用心去唱，才能够赢得观众的心，才能够赢得观众真诚的掌声。

Tuesday, September 17, 2013

The Balance

[平衡]

Balance is always beautiful. A lot of things are growing up to be strong during the process of pursuing the balance in the world. There are competitions when pursuing the balance. There is endless power of motivation when there are competitions which are promoting the reasonable development of things. Without the balance, the development of things will be irregular, and may even be uncontrolled. The power of balance is the most powerful self-controlled strength in the nature. It is the same as in our human society.

平衡永远是美丽的。这个世界的很多事物都是在追求平衡的过程中发展壮大的。有平衡才会有竞争，有竞争才会有不竭

的动力，才会推动事物良性的往前发展。失去平衡，事物的
发展将会是不规则的，甚至是不可控制的。平衡的力量是自
然界最强有力的自我控制的力量。对于我们人类社会来讲，
道理亦然。

Monday, September 9, 2013

Family - We Shall Build It Up With Our Four Hands

[家庭 – 我们应当用我们的四只手来建设]

Although we have already specified our responsibilities either in oral or in written before the couple got married, we cannot clearly refuse any housework or anything which may lie in our partner's responsibility. We need to show our love to each other. We all need to have an attitude to try to share the responsibilities as more as possible. We have established our family. We need to build it up with our four hands together. That means we are in love.

虽然情侣在结婚前已经以口头或书面的形式确定了双方的责任，但我们不可以明确拒绝本属于伴侣责任的任何家务或任何事情。我们需要显示我们的爱给对方。我们都需要有一个态度，尽量的尽可能多的分担责任。我们已经建立了我们的家庭。我们需要用我们的四只手一起来建设它。这才意味着我们在爱之中。

Monday, August 12, 2013

Politics - Society - Hardship of Single Family

[孤身血泪]

There are a large amount of single household families [one person per household] in USA and Canada, the number is quite big, this is unknown to many people, this cannot be understood by many people. For example: there are **96.6 million** unmarried Americans in USA (aged 18 and older, 2009 statistics). This group comprised **43 percent** of all U.S. residents aged 18 and older. There are **52.5 million** households maintained by unmarried men or women. These households comprised **45 percent** of households nationwide. There are **31.7 million** people who lived alone. These households comprised **27 percent** of all households.

<<Bird View>>

In Canada, there are **13, 788, 492 unmarried** population which comprised **39.53%** of all population. There are **3, 358, 125 single** household families (2006 statistics) which comprised of **27 percent** of all households in Canada.

27%, of cause is a quite huge number. I cannot understand either. The reason may lie in multiple aspects. However, the government seems to have no measures to create a perfect family for every people. Every people, as an element of the society, shall be the promoting power to create the perfect family, and should not be obstacle and fragmented power for the creation of the perfect family.

Single household family can be described as a kind of "blood and tear" hardship single. Not only to say that the solitude and loneliness suffered by the single, the housework around the room, the diet and the daily, the casual headache and fever, will obviously let people feel the desolate, let people feel the world is so helpless and incomparable sadness. I had ever seen the lonely old woman walking totteringly on the road; I had ever seen a lonely lady wondering in the tree. Such scenes are really not quite beautiful. As for the happiness of personal life, really it may not be worth to mention it.

The huge number of single household family is a serious social problem and can not but arouses our attention. Hope we all can work hard to realize such a good wish: "**Wish the world lovers get married**". Hope our society to be more harmonious and better.

在美国和加拿大有很多单身家庭[每户一人]，数字巨大，这是很多人所不了解的，也是很多人所不能够理解的。举例讲：<u>美国</u>有 **96.6 million** 未婚人士 （2009 年统计，年龄在 18 及 18 以上），占美国 18 及 18 以上总人口的 43%。 未婚家庭有 **52.5 million** （2009 年统计）， 占总家庭数目的 45%。单身家庭有 **31.7 million** （2009 年统计）， 占总家庭数目的 27%。加拿大有 **13，788，492** <u>未婚人士</u>（2012 年统计），占总人口的 39.53%。 加拿大有 **3，358，125** <u>单身家庭</u>（2006 年统计）占总家庭数目的 27%。

27%，当然是很大的数目了。 我也很难理解，原因也许是多方面的，但政府好像在这方面没有相应的举措，尽量使每个人都能够有一个完美的家庭。每一个人，作为社会的每一个分子，都应当成为完美家庭的促进力量，而不应当成为完美家庭的阻碍和割裂的力量。

单身家庭真可谓孤身血泪， 且不说孤独与寂寞，就房前屋后的家务，日常的饮食起居，偶尔的头痛与脑热都显得那么凄凄惨惨， 让人感到世间无比的悲凉。 我曾看到孤独的老人颤颤巍巍的一个人独行；我也曾看到林间独自漫步的妇人。那情景实在不是一幅很亮丽的风景线。至于说个人的幸福生活， 也许就更甭提了。

巨大数目的单身家庭是一个严重的社会问题，不能不引起我们的关注。愿大家共同努力，实现一个美好的愿望：**愿天下有情人终成眷属**。使我们的社会更和谐，更美好。

Thursday, August 8, 2013

Now and Then - Thinking on Former Yugoslavia

[此时，彼时 - 前南斯拉夫有感]

Lake Bled by Mark Gregory (https://flic.kr/p/nDjjUN)

When I see the silent water on the bled lake in Slovenia, I feel the scene is like a poem and a picture, I feel I am in the Paradise. When I see the high rising Cross on The Cathedral of Saint Sava, I can't help to be filled with emotion, I truly can't believe that an astonishing cruelty war had been happened here on this beautiful land in recent modern 90th of 20 Century. When I see their current peaceful and happy life, I truly want to get to know what is affecting the people's feelings (Love and Hate) and behaviors, and why people are getting involved in that fierce war impulsively and ruthlessly?

<<Bird View>>

Yugoslavia had been united under the leadership of **Tito** and kept its independence from both the eastern and western country groups. The people lived in a rich and happy life. The country is managed with their own management style. Maybe the overly emphasizing on the authoritativeness and fascination of personal leadership, so that errors appeared during the succession and transition of the power and authority.

Yugoslavia remind me of the hero **Walt** in the film <<Most>>, His resourcefulness and braveness, his toughness left a deep impression to countless audience. The theme song in this film <<**Bella, Ciao**>> is household renowned and can be sang nearly by everybody.

If **Tito and Walt** are still alive today, they definitely will feel sorrow and sad on their country's modern history after them.

Look again, today's Syria is quite like yesterday's Yugoslavia. I truly hope Syria's people can recover their rationale and ordinary feeling (love and hate) as quickly as possible, and come back to the peaceful and happy life. God bless them!

当我看到斯洛文尼亚 Bled Lake 那平静的湖水，恍若仙境，如诗如画的美景， 当我看到贝尔格莱德圣萨瓦大教堂那高耸的十字架，我不禁感慨万千，我真难以置信在这块美丽的土地上， 在现代文明的二十世纪九十年代曾经发生过惊人残酷的战争。看到那里人们现在和平快乐的生活，我真想搞明白

<<Bird View>>

是什么在影响人们的感情（爱与恨）和行动，人们为什么会曾经那么冲动地无情地投入到那场惨烈的战争中呢？

南斯拉夫曾经统一在铁托的领导之下，独立于东西两大阵营之外，过着富足美满的生活，管理方式也非常独特。或许是由于过于强调个人领导的权威和魅力，以致于在权力继承和交接的过程中出现差错。

南斯拉夫也令我想起电影《桥》中的主人公瓦尔特，其机智，勇敢，其铮铮铁汉的形象给无数观众留下了深刻的印象。电影主题曲《啊，朋友再见！》更是家喻户晓，人皆会唱。

如果铁托和瓦尔特今天还在的话，他们一定会为他们身后南斯拉夫的现代史而慨叹和悲伤。

再看如今的叙利亚，真得仿佛是昨日的南斯拉夫，真的希望这个国家的人民能够尽快恢复理智和平常的情感（爱与恨），回到和平快乐的生活中来。原上帝保佑他们！

Tuesday, July 30, 2013

Business: Over Sale

[商业：过度推销]

Never over sale your product or service to your customers, sell your product or service to your customers to meet their needs. Why? Because over sale will waste your customers' resource and money.

永远不要过度推销你的产品或服务给客户，推销自己的产品或服务给客户以满足他们的需求。为什么呢？因为过度推销会浪费你客户的资源和金钱。

Saturday, July 27, 2013

History - What Shall We Learn?

[历史 – 我们应当借鉴什么?]

The history of human is like a long vast river, with a remote origin and long distributions. Every time, when we look back, what shall we learn? What shall we remember? We shall learn the intelligence and wisdom of our antecessors. We shall learn the broadmindedness and humility charity of our antecessors. We shall remember each love story with a sense of heaven and earth, we shall remember each turning moment with war and peace. Reviewing history, looking back, are to help us to step out a more robust and stable step, are to prevent the replay of the historical mistakes, are to help us to have a better life today than yesterday, are to lay a better and happy life to the people of every country in the world and not only ourselves.

Reviewing history, looking back, definitely are not for remembering the hatred and hate, definitely are not for remembering the ever being defeated. If that is, we will deeply fall into the gratitude and grudges and can never free ourselves. We will stagnate in the long river of history, the level of our morality and life will never be raised.

Let's rebuild ourselves and sublimate ourselves while reviewing history and looking back!

人类历史像浩瀚的长河，源远流长。每当我们回头看我们的脚印的时候，我们应当借鉴什么？记住什么？我们应当借鉴我们前辈的聪颖和智慧，我们应当借鉴我们前辈的博大胸怀与谦卑仁爱。我们应当记住每一个感天动地的爱情故事，我们应当记住每一个化干戈为玉帛，扭转乾坤的历史时刻。回顾历史，重温历史，是为了让我们未来的脚步走得更坚实，更稳重，是为了历史的错误不再重演，是为了让我们今天的生活比昨天更美好，是为了幸福美好的生活普降于世界各国人民而不只是我们自己。

回顾历史，重温历史，决不是为了记住仇与恨，决不是为了记住曾经的失败，果真如此，我们将深陷于历史的恩恩怨怨中，无法自拔，我们将在历史的长河中徘徊不前，我们的道德和生活水平将不会提高。

让我们在回顾历史，重温历史中重塑自我，升华自我吧！

Monday, July 15, 2013

Be Yourself

[成就自我]

Be smart, be yourself, never try to be others or pretend to be others, think with your own head.

要聪明一些，要做你自己，永远不要试图成为他人或假装是他人，要用你自己的头脑来思考。

Saturday, July 6, 2013

Deep Root and Maunsell Leafs

[根深叶茂]

Big Tree by Beizhan Liu

The relationship between countries shall ground on root people, only this will ensure the stable and lasting of the relationship to withstand storm，assault and alienation. This is like a big tree with deep root to have maunsell leafs [根深叶茂].

国家与国家 之间的关系应当植根于普通百姓，只有这样才能够保证稳定而持久的关系，以抵御风暴，攻击和离间。这就好比一棵大树，只有根深才会叶茂[根深叶茂]。**(Saturday, July 6, 2013)**

Love - Get to Know Each Other

[爱 – 要相互了解]

People love the people they know, People know the people they love.

人爱其所知，人知其所爱。

Monday, July 1, 2013

Hearken

[倾听]

Only when you hearken people's inquiries, you can get to know the truth of the society, you can get to know what are there and what are not there, you can shoot out your arrow on the target, you can truly win the trust from your people.

只有倾听群众的呼声，才能洞察社会的真相。才能知所有，知所无，才能有的方矢，才能真正取信于民。

Friday, June 28, 2013

Fascination of Leadership

[领导之魅力]

The best leadership can turn enemies to be friends, turn passive situation to be active situation, influence and unite all parties which can be united, strive for and build up the best living and developing space for his organization in the complex and changeable environment.

The best leadership can get insight into the miniatures and predict the future, decide the clear direction for his organization, and adjust it to adapt the changeable environment when it is required.

The best leadership can know people and put them in the right positions, but he will not try to care everything instead of giving enough big platforms for his subordinates to play.

<<Bird View>>

The best leadership can show tender in his administration, and turn the machine like business organization to be full emotional social organization.

领导的魅力在于能够化敌为友，变被动为主动，影响并团结一切可以团结的力量，在复杂多变的环境中为自己的组织争取并营造最佳的生存及发展的空间。

领导的魅力在于能够洞察秋毫，预见未来，为自己的组织确立明确的方向，并能够适时调整以适应变化的环境。

领导的魅力在于能够知人善任，但并不事必亲工，给下属足够大的表演空间。

领导的魅力在于能够温情于政，化机器似的商业机构为有血有肉的社会组织。

Saturday, June 22, 2013

Root

[根]

Love need root. Root is based on real life's memory. Imagination cannot sustain your feeling and love.

爱需要根。根是基于现实生活的记忆。想象力是不能够维持你的感觉和爱的。

Saturday, June 22, 2013

Trying

[尝试]

Trying, only trying you can get to know something new, you can get to somewhere you never reach, and you can improve something you have. So don't be afraid of trying. You will realize your dream after continuously trying.

尝试，只有尝试，你才可以去了解新的东西，你才可以到达你从未去过的地方，你才可以完善你所拥有的东西。所以，不要害怕尝试。经过不断的尝试，你才会实现自己的梦想。

Monday, June 17, 2013

Concord Pace

[步调一致]

Marching Squad by Beizhan Liu

When we walk out alone, we can take our own steps. But when we walk in a squad, we have to step out our concord paces.

当我们独自行走的时候，我们可以把握我们自己的步伐。但是，当我们走在一个队列之中时，我们就必须迈出我们和谐一致的步伐。

Saturday, June 15, 2013

Rhythm of life

[生活的节奏]

The rhythm of life depends on our needs. We have reasons to define our own rhythm. So we can feel comfortable and happy.

生活的节奏取决于我们的需要。我们有理由来定义我们自己的节奏。我们可以因此感到舒适和快乐。

Friday, June 14, 2013

Idea

[创意]

Only good idea can lead the future of technology， only good technology can lead the future of the world. So a better world will be built upon good ideas.

只有好的创意能够引领技术的未来，只有好的技术能够引领世界的未来。因此，一个更美好的世界将构建在良好的创意之上。

Wednesday, June 12, 2013

Index

<<Bird View>>

Abbreviation

1. BRICS – Brazil, Russia, India and China and South Africa, an association of five major emerging national economies

2. UNICEF - Children's Rights & Emergency Relief Organization

3. ASEAN – Association of Southeast Asia Nations

4. APEC – Asia Pacific Economic Cooperation

5. LBJ - Lyndon B. Johnson, the 36th President of the United State

6. ARPANET – Advanced Research Projects Agency Network

7. KMT – Kuomintang, a political party in China Taiwan

8. NPC – National People's Congress, the national legislature of People's Republic of China